Praise for *Leading the Unlea*

"Alan Willett's book is timely, topical, and extremely valuable, filled with excellent examples and a great deal of practical useful wisdom."
—Prof. Barry Dwolatzky, director, Joburg Centre for Software Engineering (JCSE), Wits University, Johannesburg, South Africa

"A must read for anyone aspiring to be an exceptional leader. Alan says, "The call to leadership is a choice." If you feel called, and if you make the choice, you will glean a world of value from *Leading the Unleadable* that will benefit your career for years to come."
—David VanEpps, delivery executive, Acxiom

"When confronted by a difficult business problem, Alan can find the best bits to anchor onto and grow into team ownership. His eye for the hidden detail is second to none. Alan is a master chef and the chapters within his book are his recipes for success. Having tried a few of these recipes I can say the final dish is a delight. Alan always has a guiding manner when it seems all is lost. The calm Alan brings when acting on volatile subjects is talent we could all use. With this book I will have Alan alongside me whenever I need that advice."
—Steve Watkin, engineering director, ASM Pacific Technology

"A great addition to Alan's proven powerful contributions to the field of leadership."
—Girish Seshagiri, VP and CTO of ISHPI

"In the IT organizations I help, the root cause of most problems is a failure of leadership. I'll be handing out Alan's book to IT leaders as part of my work to help IT live up to its promise."
—Sten Vesterli, principal, More Than Code, Copenhagen, Denmark

"Thought-provoking and to the point. Alan Willett's *Leading the Unleadable* transformed how I handle difficult situations."
—Rob Synder, president & CEO, Envisage Information Systems

"Alan's work in this book is valuable at multiple levels. For all who are grappling with leadership—either as a leader, as a leader of leaders, or perhaps as an aspiring leader, he has new insights to offer. The topic is a challenging one. Alan's approach is direct and his field research really buttresses the learnings."
—Max Steinhardt, president, CBORD

"Alan provides unique guidance on how to handle the personality quirks that sometimes become big problems for the rest of the organization. Better yet, he goes well beyond reacting, to preventing the problems from even emerging. Very enriching and powerful help for leaders."

—Pedro Castro Henriques, CEO Strongstep, CEO SCRAIM

"Every work setting has its share of mavericks, cynics, divas, and other difficult people . . . The difference between success and failure is figuring out how to mold these challenging (and smart) people into one team with a common focus. Alan's book offers some great insights on how to make this happen, and he offers practical guidance and relatable examples. I recommend this book!"

—Richard Harris, executive director, Predix
Applications Engineering, GE Digital

"Alan Willett reminds us that successfully leading our organizations is all about being with people. In his book, Alan systematically deconstructs the challenges that all leaders face and lays out a playbook of pragmatic techniques and mindsets for transforming people problems into inspirational moments of leadership."

—Greg Kops, CEO, Think Topography

LEADING
THE UNLEADABLE

LEADING
THE UNLEADABLE

How to Manage Mavericks, Cynics,
Divas, and Other Difficult People

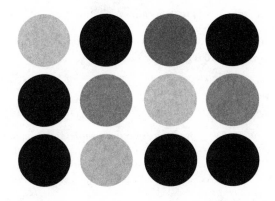

ALAN WILLETT

AMACOM

American Management Association
New York • Atlanta • Brussels • Chicago • Mexico City • San Francisco
Shanghai • Tokyo • Toronto • Washington, D.C.

This publication is designed to provide accurate and authoritative information in regard to the subject matter covered. It is sold with the understanding that the publisher is not engaged in rendering legal, accounting, or other professional service. If legal advice or other expert assistance is required, the services of a competent professional person should be sought.

Library of Congress Cataloging-in-Publication Data

Names: Willett, Alan, author.
Title: Leading the unleadable : how to manage mavericks, cynics, divas and
  other difficult people / by Alan Willett.
Description: New York, NY : AMACOM, [2016]
Identifiers: LCCN 2016017277| ISBN 9780814437605 (pbk.) | ISBN 9780814437612
  (ebook)
Subjects: LCSH: Leadership. | Problem employees. | Interpersonal conflict. |
  Conflict management. | Management.
Classification: LCC HD57.7 .W533 2016 | DDC 658.3/045–dc23 LC record available
at https://lccn.loc.gov/2016017277

About AMA
American Management Association (www.amanet.org) is a world leader in talent development, advancing the skills of individuals to drive business success. Our mission is to support the goals of individuals and organizations through a complete range of products and services, including classroom and virtual seminars, webcasts, webinars, podcasts, conferences, corporate and government solutions, business books, and research. AMA's approach to improving performance combines experiential learning— learning through doing—with opportunities for ongoing professional growth at every step of one's career journey.

10 9 8 7 6 5 4 3 2 1

This book is dedicated to my awesome family.

ACKNOWLEDGMENTS

Thank you to all my reviewers and to the leaders I interviewed. You all have provided me with great insights and helped make everything I did in this book much better.

Deborah Hazell, CEO of HSBC Global Asset Management, provided hard-hitting insights into executive leadership and challenged me to see perspectives in new ways on many topics.

Elizabeth Zach, editor at Book Crafters LLC, provided me rush services with amazing speed and clarity at the points I most needed them.

Hazel Crofts, client and friend in England, provided me with pushes on where I was missing important details and where I had injected cultural biases where they did not belong.

Jesse Schell, CEO of Schell Games, provided me with great insights into not just the special world of game design but also into getting the focus of the book narrowed in on the proper experience for my readers.

Julia Mullaney, former teammate and always a leader, gave me the big picture I needed and kept pushing me toward the high bar of excellence.

John Willig, president and literary agent at Literary Services Inc., discovered me and introduced me to the world, and kept me very focused on how to get it done!

Max Steinhardt, CEO of CBORD, was very generous with his time. Our discussions on trouble, leadership, and excellence pushed my thinking in the right directions.

Rick Harris, executive director of Application Engineering at General Electric, is one of those leaders who is like organized lightning; the speed and clarity with which he covers important topics is illuminating.

Stephen S. Power, senior editor at AMACOM, helped me shape the concept into a book with his persistence, vision, and wisdom.

Steve Watkin, director of Engineering at ASM, was one of the earliest reviewers of my materials. Thanks for being so brave!

Special thanks to my book proposal writing group led by the amazing Dr. Alan Weiss.

Special thanks to my wife, part of my two-person "duprass," who went for walks with me every time I was stuck. We covered many miles.

CONTENTS

PART 4
LEADING LEADERS   177

PREFACE

As a leader, when you have to deal with difficult people, what do you do?

- Pull them off the project?
- Chastise them in public?
- Ignore the situation and expect the team to handle it?
- Put them on a "performance improvement plan" and make it an HR problem?
- Minimize their responsibilities?
- Move them to a different group to make them someone else's problem?

Too often, leaders ignore their people problems for too long because they're afraid of conflict or, if they do act, handle the situations poorly because of inexperience or not knowing what to do. Complicating matters, the difficult people might be even more difficult to replace or the leader could have a close relationship with them.

Not acting can damage everyone around the difficult people, leading others to leave before the difficult people themselves quit. The reverse can be just as bad. Sometimes leaders terminate difficult people too quickly, which harms the group by giving it no chance to change the difficult people and reclaim them.

How you handle these situations will define you as a leader to everyone else, marking the difference between a good manager and an exceptional one.

The exceptional leader will face the problem fearlessly, directly, and quickly with the skill to transform the difficult people into the tremendous, lifting up the individual, and energizing the whole team in the process.

Throughout my career, I have been focused on learning about and pushing the boundaries of what it means to be an exceptional leader. I have worked with managers at every level from more than 100 companies in more than 15 countries, companies ranging from the large and established, such as Microsoft, Intuit, Oracle, NASA, and HP, to small start-ups. I have learned repeatedly that exceptional managers know that with great aspirations can come great difficulties. And I have learned from the bad managers how *not* to overcome those difficulties, especially the people problems. As a result, this book will show you:

- The kinds of trouble leaders face
- The measurements of success for exceptional leadership
- The principles behind the ability to handle the most troublesome situations
- How to develop the radar to spot trouble early
- How to deal with trouble
- How to prevent trouble
- How to become an exceptional leader

Exceptional leaders have one obligation above all. Whether they are managing an entire company or a team, a division, a single project, or simply a meeting, they must focus on the group, not the individual, and if an individual is hurting the group, that person must be brought back into the fold or cut out altogether. *Leading the Unleadable* is your guide to doing so.

1

THE CALL
TO EXCEPTIONAL
LEADERSHIP

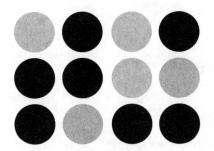

"A ship in port is safe, but that's not
what ships are built for."

—GRACE HOPPER

The Leadership Crisis Point

In working with hundreds of leaders around the world, I have found that the greater the responsibilities of leadership, the greater the amount of trouble you must deal with. Recently, a division manager responsible for 100 million dollars in revenue and 500 employees distilled the situation perfectly to a roomful of colleagues.

He held his hands a few inches apart. "This," he said, "is how much good news I get to share with the upper management of this company." He then stretched his arms the full distance. "This," he said, "is how much bad news I get to share with upper management." The other leaders in the room nodded their heads in agreement.

This is why leaders often reach the point at which they wake up one morning and simply think, "I don't want to do this anymore." They have reached a leadership crisis point. There is a way forward, though.

Many managers have called me in the midst of this crisis, often ready to hear the most important message of their leadership careers. Leadership isn't just making a series of decisions (choices) on a daily basis. The very essence of being a leader and how you lead is itself a choice.

Achieving a long, enjoyable career in management is obviously a better alternative than viewing it as a trudge across a desolate landscape of leading people who do not want to be led. The difference between these two visions of leadership is a choice that one must actively make.

You must actively embrace the many good things that come with leadership. You are in the right place to have a positive influence on others. You will be able to accomplish bigger and better things than you could accomplish on your own. You will be able to grow your own skills and abilities as you work with others, and you will gain not just from your own experience but through other people's experiences as you work with them.

Choose not just the call to leadership; choose the call to exceptional leadership. This is a call to embrace the tremendous personal growth opportunity in learning about yourself, in growing your own career, and in contributing good to the world.

Before we can listen to the call we first must understand and *accept* the following facts about leadership:

- The call to leadership is a choice.
- Whatever you lead, leadership is about leading people.
- Leadership comes with a taxonomy of trouble.
- The trouble is your fault, even when it is not.

When we accept these facts, we are ready to learn how to lead the unleadable, including our own troublesome selves.

The Call to Leadership Is a Choice

To make the step from good manager to exceptional leader, the first step is to understand that however you have found yourself in a leadership position, you have made a choice to be a leader, even if that was not your intent!

There are a number of common reasons why people find themselves in leadership positions. Each of these examples offers a short origin story that illustrates how people had to grapple with what it means personally to take on the mantle of leadership.

Promotion

Mary was superb technically, and the CEO wanted to reward her with a promotion. In Mary's company, as in many organizations, there was a ceiling to the career of the individual contributor. The only promotion available was to become a team leader. Mary happily took the promotion and the associated pay raise.

Mary had the sudden responsibility of doing work not with, but by leading, other people. She found herself doing things she had always thought of as overhead. Meanwhile, she was responsible for people doing the work she used to do. This transition was a shock to the very way Mary thought. She had to relearn how she would get meaning from her work in this new role.

Nomination Accepted

This situation happens more often than the bestowal of formal titles of leadership. There are significant issues that cut across normal boundaries in which no official leader is clearly responsible. A combination of forces happens whereby (a) someone has the skill to handle it, (b) that someone has little tolerance for the current situation, and (c) the group urges that someone to take the lead. This person may be an individual with no title but suddenly is leading.

This was actually how I became a leader. I went to college to become great at software development. Within six months in my first job, I found myself doing very little development because I was organizing and leading multiple teams that cut across organizational boundaries. I was nominated, and I accepted. Within a few months I was given the title of manager. It did take me some time before I noticed the real implications of leading people.

Business Owner

Many leaders became leaders because they had a good idea and started a business around that idea. Simon is typical of many business owners. He had a great technical idea and started a business around the idea as a business of one—just himself. However, he soon found that his idea needed other people.

Although it took a few years, Simon found himself responsible for an organization of over 300 people and growing.

Many business owners did not realize when they began their business journeys that they would be leading so many people.

A Desire for a Title

This category represents just a small percentage of all the leaders I have worked with. However, some people really want the prestige of the title that is associated with leadership. They have often received business-specific college degrees and are hungry to be part of making significant business decisions.

They reach for and achieve their desire to have the title of manager. They find much of what they expected, such as the joy of looking at the returns on significant investments they made in the course of leading their organizations. However, they are often surprised to find that there is a world of people problems that comes with leadership. They were not prepared.

The Expert Becomes Leader

This happens frequently in the field of high technology development. "The expert" has been focused on a very specialized field of the technology. Everyone begins to look to "the expert" for guidance on anything to do with that technology.

Soon, "the expert" finds himself leading a group of people who follow him easily, based on the vast knowledge he possesses. The expert is able to do his own work and guide others in theirs. The rest of the team is often essentially a pair of hands for the expert's deep understanding and vision of where the technology, and thus the team, need to go.

The trouble begins for the expert when a new technology replaces his area of expertise. This will eventually happen. Now "the expert" has been typecast as a leader but is a novice at this new technology. He is no longer the expert but still the leader and not prepared.

Dynastic Transition

This is often true in family-run organizations. The daughter or son has worked in the organization for years and now the parents step out and suddenly the heir is in charge.

For example, a friend of mine worked in his parents' company and knew that he always would. He went to college to learn about the business, then came back and was his father's go-to person for any special tasks. He worked in many areas, even on the manufacturing line when the work was so intense that his hands would help meet deadlines.

His father ran the company for another twenty years and continued to make all the important leadership decisions throughout that time.

His father retired and immediately moved to Florida, handing my friend the complete responsibility of running the company.

He was suddenly in charge.

In talking to people about their leadership origin stories, there are common experiences regardless of how they became leaders. They come to a point where they realize that the work of leadership is different. They come to the point where they realize that the work of leadership is all about people.

Further, they realize that even if they didn't mean to do so, they each made a choice to be a leader. If they faced the leadership crisis referred to in the first section and continued leading, they again made a choice.

Whatever You Lead It Is All About People

This book is written for managers and leaders of all stripes. But what do they lead?

Leading a Group of Leaders Within a Company

This is a generic category that can include, for example, the COO (Chief Operating Officer) or a division leader of a cast of hundreds. Or it can include a manager of a group of thirty. The common characteristic is that they are leading other leaders.

These leaders report to at least one other person and often have a cast of stakeholders who have high expectations of results.

Leading Projects

The leader here may have a very large project team. There are teams as large as a thousand people dedicated to developing and delivering a single product to the marketplace. There are also teams as small as just two people.

The project leader must deliver results, whether anyone reports to her directly or not. She may have a single sponsor who is paying for the project. It is, however, more likely that the project has many stakeholders who care about those results, and they often have conflicting priorities they are presenting to that project leader.

Leading a Company

This can range from leading a famous company such as Apple to helming a small restaurant with a staff of three. It can also include a company the size of one person where individuals must lead themselves but also a virtual team of everyone who helps support that company, such as lawyers and accountants.

Even CEOs who are in charge of an entire company, small or large, have a number of stakeholders outside their direct lines of command. This can include the board of directors, a board of advisers, and investors in the company. It also always includes the customers of the business.

Leading a Cause

Gandhi, Martin Luther King, Jr., and many others are examples of people who had no official position but are yet considered great leaders.

I have a number of friends who are activists. One person is specifically working to protect the fresh water in our local lakes. She has put many hours into speaking, writing, and organizing to achieve this mission. She has suddenly found herself a leader of many people, none of whom are paid. Nor does anyone officially work for her. Yet all of these people look to her for leadership.

• • •

The common thread all the examples have is that leaders are leading other people to accomplish a shared set of objectives. The objectives vary immensely across the various roles of leadership and the context within which the leaders work, but what they all have is a set of responsibilities that comes with leadership.

These responsibilities are not to just get things done, but to lead others to accomplish great tasks.

All leaders know that it is truly all about leading people, and that comes with a taxonomy of trouble.

Leadership Comes with a Host of Trouble

A friend of mine once said, "Everything was fine until there was more than just me in the room." That evoked my laughter because he was talking about me entering the room—a great joke!

However, I often remember his quote when I find myself in a room full of discord. Yet, we absolutely need others if we wish to achieve the bigger things we desire to accomplish.

The following is a taxonomy of difficult challenges that leaders, even those with just a few years of leadership experience, are likely to encounter.

Troublesome Project Teams

If a project is truly striving for exceptional impact, there is a level of stress on the team and natural barriers in the way of success. This is normal. The problem occurs when the project's troubles start negatively impacting the whole organization. Consider these three examples.

1. **Teams that are always late and have quality issues.** This occurs when the project team says they are "almost done" and then announces to management that they need another three months. When that time is almost up, they say that they need yet another three months. This delays the revenue expected from this project repeatedly and does not allow the organization to plan. Quality issues exacerbate these delays. Further, this impacts the ability of leadership to start other projects and thus delays the revenue achieved from these other projects.

2. **The "firefighting" projects.** These teams are constantly battling fires. They release their products to their customers, but there are always significant problems that the team must deal with. The problems are multiplicative, typically starting with phone calls from customers. Further, the team is spending so much time fighting fires that the time to build new services or features is greatly diminished.

3. **The divided team.** There will be stress on any team striving for excellence, and that often leads to conflict. The key is that conflict must be constructive such that arguments produce

better solutions and improved trust. With the wrong chemistry, the opposite occurs, resulting in damaged trust and team drama. The worst variant of this situation is when that drama leaks from the project in trouble and divides other parts of the organization as well. The damage done has many ripple effects, as leaders have to deal with drama instead of progress.

Troublesome Individuals

Projects such as the ones just mentioned can get in trouble because of things like technology issues or incorrect requirements. However, those are often excuses. Projects are successfully completed by people—not by methodology or technology. If a project is in trouble it is most likely to be a people issue.

The following is a sample of people issues that leaders commonly must address.

The cynic. Sarcasm, cynicism, pessimism, whining, and general sniping are all common negative attitudes that, when delivered in the right-sized doses, can provide relief to difficult situations. However, many leaders have faced situations where individuals bring too much of that attitude to the team and it breaks down the fabric of the team culture.

The slacker. Many times, managers face the problem of an individual not living up to teamwork standards. There can be many causes for this, but the main problem facing the leader is that there is a team member who is not contributing sufficient value. This is sometimes a competence problem, sometimes a bad fit of skill to task, and sometimes an attitude problem where someone just doesn't seem to care. The appearance may be "slacking," but the causes behind it are often hidden.

The diva. Some people are experts at narcissism. It appears that they believe that everything that is going on is all about them. In fact, with the most extreme divas, if things happen that distract from the diva being the center, the diva will raise enough trouble to bring the spotlight firmly back to his or her own personal center-stage performance. This is often a difficult leadership challenge, as most people develop their diva personalities because they are actually very good at what they do.

The pebble in the shoe. These people are the teammates who provide persistent annoyance to other teammates. The types of annoyances vary. Sometimes a person has a ready excuse that is actually plausible, but it seems there is always an excuse. Another example is the person who is a little critical of other teammates, with comments ranging from their clothes to how the work is done. It isn't quite enough to challenge them on it; it is the persistence of it. These slights observed by an outsider for one day would seem to be just mildly annoying if noticed at all. Yet these little "bug bites" being repeated daily have a cumulative negative effect.

Troublesome Leaders

If you are a leader of leaders, you may have all the troubles previously listed. You are also likely at some point to face any of these additional situations.

Clash of the titans. People in leadership positions are generally very ambitious, which means there will be conflicts over such things as direction of the group, desire for the same resources, or who gets which set of offices. People in leadership positions are also likely to be collaborative, however, so these conflicts should be manageable. Nevertheless, at some point you will be faced with a leadership group composed of people actively trying to make each other fail. They are engaged in destructive conflict, which if not addressed will adversely affect the whole company.

The maverick. Many executives consistently try to push themselves and their organizations to higher levels. Thus, they often seek managers who will bring fresh ideas to the organizations to push past the status quo. This backfires when the new leader is a maverick who is ready to throw away all of the status quo. The leader is suddenly faced with a culture clash between the maverick and the rest of the organization. In these situations, the leader has many people saying, "If the maverick is staying, I am leaving."

Leaders facing their own leadership crises. The other challenge leaders of leaders must be aware of is that the leaders they lead are feeling the burdens of responsibility. An individual team member who suddenly quits has an impact. When a manager suddenly departs, there is a much larger and longer-term impact. As leaders, we must watch for these moments and be ready to help those leaders across their own crises.

Troublesome Stakeholders

As a leader at any level, you have responsibilities to the people you are leading, as well as the people who are stakeholders. This is even true for chief executives who report to a board of directors, and if not to the board of directors then to their customers. Here are three examples of that kind of trouble.

1. **Too many bosses with conflicting priorities.** As a leader, it is likely you have many stakeholders and that your direct manager, if you have one, is just one of them. When you have multiple stakeholders, it is rare for those stakeholders to agree on what your top priority is. Leaders who do not know how to handle the problem of multiple stakeholders with conflicting priorities have trouble brewing every morning before they even start their own coffee brewing.

2. **The wrong level of involvement from your stakeholders.** The trouble here can be when your stakeholders want to micromanage not just you but also the people who work for you. Just as damaging can be the invisible stakeholders. You need their attention and they are nowhere to be found. It is not just that the stakeholders are invisible to you; you are also invisible to them. When you have critical needs, they won't hear you. Yet when you don't deliver, the trouble is still yours.

3. **Irrational pressure from above.** I once talked to a project manager who was in charge of a large software development project of over 100 people. I asked her when the first major deliverable would be made. When she answered June 15, which was four months away, her voice was tense. I asked her if it could possibly be delivered earlier. She looked stricken and said very loudly, "no!" I asked her if there was a chance it could be delivered later, and she again answered "no!"

It is not possible to plan significant projects with that much precision. Her reaction was because the management above her was putting great pressure on making that date.

Bright-light projects bring lots of pressure. Much of it does come from above. However, much of it is also self-imposed. This pressure leads to bad decisions and late surprises.

All of this has one significant common attribute. That attribute brings us to the last place trouble can come from: you.

The Trouble Is Your Fault, Even When It Is Not

"It was my responsibility. Thus, as far as anybody was concerned, it was my fault." Watts told me this one day on our morning run.

When I worked with Watts Humphrey, recipient of the National Medal of Technology from President George W. Bush, he often told stories about his challenges in leadership, especially during our morning runs before we started our workdays.

During this run, Watts was telling the story about taking over responsibility for a very large project at IBM. He took over a project where he became the leader of leaders of a project involving over a thousand people.

On the first day, he found out how seriously behind schedule the project was. He told me that he thought hard about the problem and then, laughing, he said "I asked who was to blame, and I realized that really there was only one person to blame and that was me. It didn't matter to anyone that it was only my first day. On that first day it became my responsibility. Thus, as far as anybody was concerned, it was my fault."

Watts was partially kidding about the problem being his fault. His real point was that blame has nothing to do with troublesome situations. If you are the leader responsible for making sure the mission is accomplished, if it is not accomplished, it is still your responsibility.

This may seem obvious, but the following common behaviors demonstrate that too many are slow to reach this acceptance of responsibility. Which of these have you seen or perhaps even can identify with?

It is not really a problem. When confronted with a schedule problem, the quick reaction is "We are not really that far behind." When seeing a serious quality issue, the quick response is "Well, it only happened in this one place, this one instance."

It is not our problem. The excuses come quickly when the leader can point to others. "The third-party vendor was late with the deliverable" or "The customer provided us with unachievable conflicts in the requirements."

We need time to put into place this new set of tools. It could be a new set of tools. It could be a new magic methodology such as rapid prototyping or "lean agile." If we have these things everything will be better (we hope).

This is an especially hard problem and it takes time. To be most annoying, this must be said in a whiny voice.

Anyone of these excuses can be absolutely valid. However, these are simply excuses and when said in those ways it is done to deflect responsibility. Further, it absolutely delays the most effective solutions to the problems at hand.

Note that these excuses are common even among good managers. Those managers do get the work done, eventually, except when they don't. It is also these good managers who often face the leadership crisis we mentioned at the start of the chapter.

They haven't yet crossed the Rubicon to know that to become an exceptional leader it is about more than seeing to things getting done. It is a choice to accept that leadership is all about leading people to achieve more than they believed was possible. It is about accepting that all high-impact projects come with troublesome project teams, people, leaders, and stakeholders.

You must accept that those troubles are your responsibility.

One of the keys that made Watts an exceptional leader was his ready acceptance of this fact followed by his willingness to directly deal with the trouble. He had to bring his various team leaders and management above into the solution, but the solution started with accepting responsibility for it.

To successfully lead the unleadable, we must accept that leadership is a choice. Further, we can choose the kind of leaders we desire to be.

REFLECTION POINTS

For maximum personal benefit, take a few minutes to answer these questions out loud or to write your answers down.

1. What was your pathway to leadership? Did you set out to lead people?

2. How often with how much impact have you encountered the taxonomy of trouble?

3. Are you facing any of that trouble now or see it coming soon?

   - Troublesome project teams?
   - Troublesome individuals?
   - Troublesome leaders?
   - Troublesome stakeholders?

4. Which of the following phrases have you recently used? Which one did you use most often?

   - It is not really a problem.
   - It is not our problem.
   - We need time to put into place this new set of tools.
   - This is an especially hard problem and it takes time.
   - It is my responsibility. I will ensure we remedy the situation and put in measures to prevent this in the future.

2

Accept the Call of
Exceptional Leadership

---

had my leadership crisis about twenty-five years ago.

It occurred when I was a leader in a division of Xerox at the height of its powers. The pressures on me were enormous, both from the managers and stakeholders above and around me and from my team of people, who expected my guidance, protection, and help with their own advancements.

In addition to working to help my team achieve a large list of goals and deadlines, I was also leading multiple cross-organizational task forces. The days were long. I accomplished much, but the list of things that I believed should have been accomplished on any one day felt like it always overwhelmed any of those victories.

On top of this, I found that I did not value the work I was doing. I did not find joy in it. I once ran an ultramarathon on trails in the spring. It was a long, cold slog through creeks that went up to my waist, crawling up mud hills and sliding down the other sides, hitting rocks on the way down. In some ways this was similar to work with two big differences. I enjoyed all the challenges of the ultramarathon and, unlike work, that actually did have a finish line.

I decided I could not continue in this way. I went into my office and closed the door. I canceled all my meetings. I ignored all phone calls. This was a problem that I would solve. Through the week, I contemplated many things. The following were the most important realizations.

- Growing up on a farm, I learned much about business and leadership. I especially learned from my parents that work is a choice and making the choice was a key component of joy. My father would laugh when he read about people retiring to farming after waiting for years to do so. He loved farming and found it strange that people would wait so long to do what they love.

- I looked to the future and contemplated what my next fifty years would be like. There were many things I realized thinking that far into the future. The limits of our time on this Earth was one clear realization on that not-so-distant horizon, but also an opening of my mind to a plethora of opportunities ahead if I used my imagination. If I chose courage.

- Many of the things I was doing for my job were things that I did not believe were right for the company. I was asked to do them, but that didn't mean these were the right things. I knew for sure that many of the things I was doing and how I was doing them were not right for me.

- I realized that the mental model I had of my job as an endless marathon of slogging through mud was simply my projection onto the situation. I was choosing that mindset.

By the time that I left work on Friday, I had quit working for Xerox, but I didn't tell anyone because I didn't need to—I simply quit the mental model of the job I held in my head. I realized that from that point onward I was going to work for the same person I had been working for all along but didn't realize it.

I was going to work for me. It did not mean I would waiver in my commitment to Xerox. Instead, I was taking ownership of providing the best value I could contribute to my company and its customers. The difference was my taking ownership of that contribution and how to best achieve it.

In the years since that transformative crises point, I have spoken to many other leaders who came to the same conclusion when they faced and overcame their leadership crises. Although the details vary with our paths, the pattern is clear.

After we realized with great clarity that our career belonged to each of us as individuals, we returned to work on a different mission.

We had chosen the path of exceptional leadership.

What Does It Mean to Choose Exceptional Leadership?

The first thing it meant for me was that I chose it.

I had realized that the main difference between the muddy ultramarathon and my work life was simply that: choice. I had chosen to run the muddy horrendous hills of the ultramarathon and although it was often difficult, and sometimes painful, I found the thing to be fun and rewarding. Meanwhile, I was treating my work life as an obligatory trudge across a desolate landscape.

I was finding work difficult because I was being a victim. I was not choosing to be there. My big realization was that my mindset was simply wrong. Every day that I went to work was a choice. No one was forcing me at gunpoint to go there. Further, I realized my work life could be full of fascinating, rewarding challenges.

It was up to me.

When I returned to work on Monday, as far as anyone else knew, I had returned to the same job with the same set of responsibilities. They were not completely wrong. I did have the same title. I still had those responsibilities.

However, my person mental model had changed. I was now treating myself as a business of one person who was choosing to provide services to my employer in exchange for the company's choice to pay me. In running this business of "me," I had three significant mindset shifts.

1. **Provide great return on investment to my employer.** For me to be successful, my employer must be successful. Thus, my focus was changed from "get stuff done" to "have great positive impact on the business."

2. **Improve me.** Any business must be focused on the now and on the future. My new mindset changed to think of every investment in time I made as having to be beneficial to my employer *but also to myself.* I wanted everything to be a clear learning opportunity that provided value to me and my employer. Before this goal, improvements of my skill set were secondary to getting the job done. I promoted this to be equal in value.

3. **Reduce my labor while dramatically increasing the value I provide.** Before this mindset shift, I just worked harder, whatever the challenge was. The more tasks that came my way, the harder I worked, and I was rewarded generously with more tasks. My focus on providing value with impact changed how I treated every single request that came my way.

I recently discussed these mindset shifts with a business owner. Even as a business owner he was not immune to being "run by the business" as opposed to him "running the business." Our leadership crisis stories had parallels. He too found himself on a repetitive treadmill of just working harder. We both had come to the conclusion that we needed to focus our time on the big benefits to ourselves and the businesses.

These mindset shifts result in significant changes in how leaders approach work. Here are five examples of how to manifest the changes in day-to-day work.

1. **Make "What are the business goals and benefits?" a favorite question.** Any time that a stakeholder approaches you, including a direct manager, or any of your employees has an idea for more work, always initiate a discussion that starts with that question.

2. **Do not allow micromanagement of the how.** Focus on the best way you know to achieve the goals. This may seem obvious, but many of my clients work with micromanagers who are challenged in their abilities to clearly state their goals; they instead want to dictate what tasks to do and how to do them. The micromanagers think they want a pair of hands, but accepting that diminishes the results. I simply refused to work this way, often to the micromanagers' shock, as no one else did this. I would talk with them until I understood the goals and then I would say, "If I achieve the goals, do you really care how I get it done?" Freedom in *how to achieve* the goals improves the efficiency and the results.

3. **Seek opportunities to dramatically improve your business.** This is a big shift for most people. Before the mindset shift, they were so overwhelmed that they would never consider looking for *more* work. With the mindset shift, you will be thinking

about the overall business and where you can provide the most impact. You will be pitching new ideas and initiatives that further the business of you, and the business that you own or are employed by.

4. **Make saying "no" become valuable to you and others.** In spite of loads of literature and coaching on the importance of "no," many people still find this challenging. If you focus on the business and where your effort can provide the most impact, the word *no* becomes almost effortless. I admit that my manager was initially startled by my sudden change in this regard. However, he soon came to understand that whenever I said "no" it was in his best interest.

5. **Cut your "nonsense tolerance" level significantly.** Before my mindset shift, I was doing lots of work I just didn't care about, and too much of it fit into the "this work is balderdash" category. Before my mindset shift, roughly 50 percent of my activities fit into that category. After the shift, I worked relentlessly to keep it under 10 percent.

I really enjoyed the ultramarathons that I raced in. All of these changes added up to making work into as much fun as those races were for me. Work became challenging and rewarding. I now shaped the daily challenges to be rewarding for my employer and myself. Everyday I went to work I knew it was my choice.

The most invigorating part of this change was based on a conscious choice of how to shape my work to fit within exceptional leadership and the associated measurements of success.

Success Measures of Leadership

For those who have accepted the call to leadership, the initial mission they take on is simple: Get more done by leading people to accomplish even more than they could accomplish alone.

The best and simplest measure of successful leadership is results because results matter. Here are the typical indicators of success for this.

> ► **Make a profit.** The executives of any significantly sized organization are keenly aware that the lifeblood of their organization is making profits. Further, they must delegate much of the day-to-day operations to other members of the organization. They do this so they can focus on *next year's* profit. They are aware that the actions they take will define whether payroll can be met not just this year, but next year and beyond.

> ► **Deliver on time.** The standard in most project management literature is delivering projects on time with high-quality results. This is often hard to do, especially when working in the world of new technologies. In spite of how hard it may be, that difficulty is never an accepted excuse. Delivering on time with high quality *is* a measure of success. If you do not deliver to expectations, projects will not be deemed as successful. You will not be deemed as successful.

> ► **Delight customers and inspire loyalty.** Whether you are a leader with the title of CEO or the title of project manager, it is well known that the result that really counts is providing great value to your customers.

Without delivering value you will not make a profit. In fact, it must be value that delights and inspires loyalty of the customer to the brand.

Successful leaders get things done. Their businesses are successful. They deliver. They make a profit. And these leaders do this in spite of all the troubles that plague them.

Many managers are successful in this way, but the call to exceptional leadership can take them to a higher level of achievement.

Success Measures of Exceptional Leadership

The first difference with exceptional leaders is that they have a very personal, passionate mission that goes beyond those simple (and, yes, important) results. Thus, their measures of success also have a much higher bar. Consider these famous leaders and ask yourself if they would be satisfied with simply the results in the previous section.

- Steve Jobs, who said, "We're here to put a dent in the universe. Otherwise, why else even be here?"
- Susan B. Anthony, who worked tirelessly for decades in support of women's right to vote. She was often derided and even arrested. A woman's right to vote was ratified four years after her death.
- John F. Kennedy, who initiated the mission to the moon and said, "We choose to go to the moon in this decade and do the other things, not because they are easy, but because they are hard."

Exceptional leadership calls for exceptional measures that go beyond the simple measures of profit or on-time delivery. The following are criteria that exceptional leaders employ that are useful and inspiring.

Measure the Positive Difference for Your Customers

For a project to be successful, the customer must like it well enough to use it. In the history of software development, many products delivered became "shelf ware," where people bought it and never used it. For the simple measure of short-term profit this is fine. For most, this bar of success is sufficient.

However, having customers use your product is a simple, important measure. It is even better to have your customers be delighted. This is good in a twofold way. First, your product is making an important difference for your customers. Second, they are much more likely to buy more products in the future.

Track the Attrition Rates of Top Talent

Since executives know that their results are truly based on the talents, loyalties, and focus of other people, one of the key measures they watch is attrition. And although they care about the attrition of the overall organization, the exceptional leader is especially focused on retaining the top talent of the organization. If you are keeping your top talent, it is likely you are creating an environment where they thrive.

Measure Whether Constructive Conflict Occurs Much More Often than Destructive Conflict

Exceptional leaders understand that if you are pushing for excellence, pushing on boundaries of the status quo, conflict will occur. Some organizations have a hard time distinguishing between constructive and destructive conflict. Destructive conflict becomes more about the people than the idea. It breaks down trust even if a good idea emerges. The lost trust creates more conflict.

Constructive conflict builds on ideas and will actually build more trust between people. Constructive conflict creates energy, passion, and greater belief in the team.

What is the ratio of constructive versus destructive conflict in your organization?

Watch to Ensure That the Energy Equation Is Positive

One of the measures my best clients use when leading their critical projects is the "energy equation." Are you ready for high math? During checkpoints for the project, the question is asked, "Is the energy you are getting out of doing this project greater than the energy you are putting in?" I have personally worked on projects where it seemed the project was draining so much energy from me that it felt that it could eat my soul! Okay, that is an exaggeration, but you see the point. The high bar for projects should be that the personal energy equation of the team is very positive.

Watch the Trend Lines of Unacceptable Behaviors or Results

Exceptional leaders will have clearly defined what excellence is. They will also have been clear about the behaviors that are unacceptable. How many times do you hear about trouble in these areas? How many times is it related to a specific person or team? Is this decreasing or increasing over time? Are the actions you are taking working to improve the situation or the opposite?

Measure Your Troublesome to Tremendous Conversion Rate

An important measure in the game of baseball is a player's batting average. Baseball players that hit above .300 are considered heroes. Consider how many times you have had the opportunity to help someone fix negative interactions with a group. How many were fully successful and how many failed? How many times have you had to deal with projects that were in trouble and transformed them into tremendous? As with baseball players facing pitchers who throw over 90 miles per hour, these situations are often difficult. However, success is possible. How wonderful it is for you and the team when your conversion rate is high!

Watch Your Protégés Excel

Truly, the best measure of exceptional leadership is seeing the people who have learned from that leader. If you have had the pleasure to coach, mentor, and guide a number of people who have gone on to be highly successful, you can certainly take great pleasure in knowing that you were part of their journeys. If they still seek your counsel it is a very good indicator that your leadership is exceptional.

Accepting the Call of Exceptional Leadership

I took my daughter to a driving course where the students got to drive cars on a closed course that mimicked the worst conditions drivers might face on the road. One challenge had the drivers go at high speeds into a slick surface to learn how to get a car out of a skid. One of the students simply took his hands off the wheel when this happened and said "Oh My!" He did this three times before he figured out that if he could not actually control the car, he could at least influence it into the right direction!

Some people stand on the brink of the call to exceptional leadership and back away. They back away because of fear of the responsibility of accepting that call.

Somehow they find it easier to be able to continue to play the victim. Essentially, these leaders throw up their hands from their steering wheels and say they have no control over their problems with their customers, their managers, the technology, or those unleadable people they were allegedly leading. They refuse to keep their hands on the steering wheels.

They choose that desolate landscape of no control, which they said they were unhappy with. The familiar is more comfortable to them than the difficultly that the changes require.

Accepting the call to exceptional leadership does come with new challenges and new responsibilities. It isn't always easy. Here are five things to do to help meet the challenges.

1. **Be fearless.** That is easier said than done, and you must work at it. If your journey is similar to mine, when you start saying "no" to things you used to say "yes" to, the reactions can vary and even include anger. Nonetheless, saying "no" will often be the right choice. Be fearless and confident in your choice.

2. **Build *your* own community of exceptional leaders.** Leaders who choose this path notice that there are not many people who have chosen this path, but they can immediately identify the leaders who have. Talk to them, work with them, and learn from them.

3. **Stop whining.** That is obvious and still worth saying. It is fine to take the occasional whine break, but make it short. In the middle of the ultramarathons I run, occasionally another runner and I take a moment to compare the pains of the activity we are engaged in. We then laugh and get back to the work at hand. The best people to have a whine break with are other exceptional leaders. Make it quick, though; we don't have much patience for it!

4. **Learn to love the challenge of transforming the troublesome to the tremendous.** This is the opposite of the whining that perhaps you used to do! When you have a difficult employee who is challenging you, learn to relish this as an opportunity to grow others and yourself in the process.

5. **Know that learning will have setbacks.** Taking on brand new learning opens up pathways in your mind and is very exciting. There will be moments, though, where it is a more difficult path than the familiar one. Take your time and learn the new road. It is worth the effort.

Perhaps you are already doing these activities. If so, congratulations, as you are either already an exceptional leader or you are well on your way. If you are not doing them, consider the choice that you have. Only by leading your unleadable self can you then prepare to lead the unleadable.

REFLECTION POINTS

Leadership is ultimately a choice. Exceptional leadership is also a choice. Engaging in this choice is a personal journey where it is best to think about what choices you make for yourself that are helpful to you and to others. I encourage you to take a few minutes to try to answer the following questions.

1. What is your mission as a leader? Why have you chosen leadership?

2. How do you know if you are being successful as a leader? What are your indicators of success?

3. How will you being an exceptional leader benefit others?

4. How do others view you as a leader? How do you know?

The Mindset to Lead
the Unleadable

P eople who practice mindful meditation maintain that it changes their mindset and that change in how they think leads to different, improved behaviors. Scientists such as Sara Lazar, Ph.D., of the Massachusetts General Hospital Psychiatric Neuroimaging Research Program have reinforced those anecdotal claims by showing through brain studies that the physical brain actually changes as well.

Changing *how* we think physically changes us!

Championship athletes frequently discuss how they work hard on their bodies and also on their mindsets. Jack Nicklaus, who won a record eighteen professional major golf championships, speaks often about how he visualized his every shot before he stepped to the golf tee: "I 'see' where I want it to finish, nice and white and sitting high on the bright green grass." My favorite quote by Muhammad Ali is "I am the greatest. I said that even before I knew I was." That is the quintessential representation of mindset in that it defined clearly in his mind how he would think about himself and represent himself to the world.

When we change our mindsets that changes how we act in response to the events that occur around us. How we act changes the outcomes. To be able to best manage the mavericks, cynics, divas, and other difficult people and situations, we have to first change our frames of reference in how we think about them.

This chapter describes the key elements of the mindset for leading the unleadable.

• KEY #1 •

Appreciate The Diversity Of Every Leaf

I really enjoy going for long walks or runs through the trails, woods, gorges, and general wildness that surrounds where I live. What amazes me is how in spite of many plants' similarities, close inspections reveal that each one is different. Even if you inspect the leaves on a single tree, you will find differences among the leaves.

When I travel around the world to other forests, deserts, canyons, and all the diversity I find our world has to offer, it just becomes more amazing.

The same is true when I work with various organizations around the world. I find that, as in nature, the diversity of culture is a rich, textured tapestry of where we have all come from with our unique backgrounds.

When I work with teams in India I find different thought processes than when I do work in South Africa. When I do work with teams in San Diego, California, I find they work differently from teams in New York City.

Besides the different experiences people have due to growing up male or female, research shows that male and female brains are hardwired in different ways such that males and females actually think differently.

Exceptional leaders more than understand this diversity, they love it! First, it is important to recognize that we all have similarities that have great value. Communication could not happen at all without that! The secret is to understand that the diversity that always exists produces some "noise" in our communications.

When someone speaks to another person, each sentence has a unique context that includes their own background, how they think about things, how they learned the language in which they speak, and their assumptions about the current circumstance. When another person listens to that person they go through all of their own filters that are different from those of the person speaking. The more differences among their filters, such as growing up in a different country or in a different economic strata, the more likely that the differences between the meaning the speaker intended and the meaning the listener heard are significant.

This noise can cause confusion or, worse, lead to mistaken assumptions that lead to anger.

This is important! Exceptional leaders know that when encountering some behavior or action that appears unacceptable, their first thought should be to wonder what they don't understand about the person and the communication process.

Good managers can miss big things because with their cultural filters, these things are invisible. Consider what I witnessed in an organization that was predominately one ethnicity, and almost all male. In a team setting, a woman points out the problems with an approach. She does so clearly and bluntly. She is ignored. Later, often two or three meetings later, a male points out the same problem, and someone says, "Oh, good catch."

In sharp contrast to this are organizations that have immense diversity and also typically have diversity training. There are not only significantly more female team members, but also women in leadership positions. When I see a woman perform the same actions in such a group she is immediately listened to. She is viewed by leadership as an innovative thinker who speaks her mind. In fact, she often is the team leader.

Note that the difference is not just better for women. It is also much better for the group and organization, as the diversity of thinking accelerates idea development and innovation for the customers served. Having multiple ways of thinking about things can lead to arguments, but with great leadership this results in great innovation.

• KEY #2 •

Start with the Belief That Everyone Has Good Intentions

Most people actually have good intentions and are working toward what they believe is the greater good of the organization. Even if they are annoying, or doing things that you believe are counter to the good of the organization, it is unlikely that they are damaged, stupid, or evil.

When confronted with difficult situations, especially situations that seem directly related to troublesome behaviors or attitudes, this is an especially important mindset to have ingrained as your first response.

A friend of mine worked for a short time in an organization where the owner exploded with anger any time something went wrong. By the end of the day, it was common for someone to have his employment with the company terminated either because the owner fired him, or the person on the receiving end of the anger quit. The company lasted for only two short years in spite of having started with very good products and an enthusiastic customer base.

This is an extreme example, but it does demonstrate the impact of reacting improperly to bad news.

Many leaders are very driven to achieve great results. It is natural to have a strong reaction to bad news or the perception that someone is not driven in the same way that you are. In coaching these leaders to work toward a more constructive response, I urged them to find the mindset that drove them to this reaction. The most common answer these leaders came up with was "when things went wrong, my initial gut reaction was that troublesome people were trying to cause me or the organization harm" and it was that belief that made them feel such negative emotions. When they articulated this feeling it became apparent that this was actually never true in any of the situations they faced.

The exceptional leader believes that when someone is causing problems it is not the person's intention to cause problems. Almost certainly the troublesome person is trying to do his or her best to further the overall good of the initiative. The calm leader has the mindset that when trouble arises, it is not of evil intent, it is because something is missing.

The "angry" leaders I worked with did change their mindsets. This change in mindset does not mean we ignore bad behaviors or bad results. What it does mean is that when confronted with these situations we immediately have a more focused, constructive response.

This calm response, followed by more actions, is described later in this book.

• KEY #3 •

Accept Reality But Do Not Let Reality Define You

Steve Jobs set a high bar. According to Walter Isaacson's biography of Jobs, the president of Corning told Jobs that it wasn't possible to meet the deadlines he had in mind. Jobs said, "Don't be afraid. You can do this." In this instance and many others, Steve Jobs was not going to let the "reality" before him define him. He would push to change it. Corning delivered Gorilla Glass in time for the iPhone launch.

Exceptional leaders do push to set a high bar, and to define what that high bar should be. This takes an important mindset, which is summed up in the threefold relentless pursuit of seeing reality, accepting reality, and, based on this, dealing with reality in a way that sets a high standard of achievement.

See Reality

Observation, questioning, and reflection are incredibly important keys to leadership. If you are unable to determine the reality of the situation within and surrounding your very important initiative, the initiative is at great risk! The better you are at determining the current reality and predicting future reality if things continue, the better your ability to not let the current reality define the outcome.

Explore the details within your domain. Ensure that you have data that is accurate, useful, and used. Develop the ability to focus on the most important elements. For example, be able to rise above the daily noise of problems and excuses. Be able to see patterns and trends and understand when the indicators call for clear action.

I have worked with many projects that have had critical deadlines. For example, I have worked with projects at the company Intuit where if you missed a deadline, you missed the tax season. It was critical to the team to have detailed data to let them know on a daily basis if they were on track, so they could make real-time adjustments. The data would let them know very clearly, and all too often, that they were going to miss that deadline unless they took action.

Accept Reality

This step is difficult for many. It is perhaps too easy to listen to those who say, "It will get better" or even to tell that to yourself. We can easily choose to say "We are actually okay because . . . " This list usually includes that the project had a special event that won't be repeated or that the hard part was done first and the rest will be easy.

Ah, it would be so nice to believe that. However, it is so rarely true.

Exceptional leadership looks at these details but does not accept the notion that working harder will fix everything. Instead, exceptional leaders study the details for more complete understanding and are thus prepared for determining the next step.

Returning to the Intuit example, the projects I worked with often had indicators of being behind. Teams that ignore those problems end up missing their deadlines. Instead of just accepting that the data was right or wrong, this team studied it and applied their engineering judgment. They accepted what they saw and prepared to act.

Do Not Let Reality Define the Outcome

This final step is a tough one too because dealing with reality usually includes publicly admitting problems and soliciting help. For the example of a quality problem, exceptional leaders will push themselves and others to investigate every opportunity to improve the situation. Further, they will engage with others beyond the project as well. They will not allow the current reality to be the definitive outcome. Exceptional leaders relish this step because they know that dealing with reality is the only way to achieve excellent results.

In the Intuit example, one of the projects I was dealing with found a significant issue where it would have been natural to ask management to drop a feature to be able to make the deadline. However, the team leader encouraged the team to not let the data define the outcome for them. The team engaged in multiple brainstorming sessions and came up with solutions. They were also not afraid to apply extra sweat and to ask for help from other teams. They achieved their deadline with style.

See reality. Accept reality. Deal with reality.

None of these steps are simple or easy, but pursuing them is a far better path than the alternative.

• KEY #4 •

Set the High Bar for Excellence That People Desire

We're used to defective software, whether it causes our computers to hang or enables a hacker to exploit it. Nonetheless, we accept this state of affairs because "software has bugs. It is the nature of the business."

There is only a little truth to that. Many teams do struggle with software quality, but some deliver large complex systems of software with very high quality results and zero operational defects.

The leaders of these two types of teams have different mindsets.

The leaders of the high-quality results organization know that people crave the high bar of doing excellent work.

If this seems obvious to you then you may already have this mindset. However, in conducting many organizational assessments I have not found this mindset to be pervasive; instead, I have found the opposite.

In conducting organization assessments I have the benefit of talking to all layers of large and small organizations, from CEOs to individual contributors. When I ask about disappointments, the most common answer I hear is "We didn't take the time to do the job with quality."

That was the case with most organizations, but there were organizations that were exceptions. In those exceptional organizations, disappointment around quality was not in anyone's answer. Not one person! Because I typically heard it so often, I knew there was something different in those organizations.

The following demonstrates the mindset of excellence by contrasting the common themes in these two very different types of leadership.

The Low Bar

The leadership in these organizations may actually be driving very hard toward results. However, the way in which they drive toward results is the antithesis of going for excellence. Here are some actual quotes from leaders in these organizations.

- "Get this new software development project to testing as soon as possible. We have to start finding the defects."
- "We don't have budget nor time for training."
- "I don't care about your concern for quality. All I care about is the date. Make it happen."
- "Don't talk to Hank, our most important developer, about those quality problems. He might get angry."

There is a mindset that underlies these quotes. In this example, the leadership expects through their words and actions that the development team will deliver poor quality to testing and it is testing's job to fix it.

These leaders believe that quality is expensive and will slow productivity. They also believe that people cannot achieve excellent results and actually may get upset and quit if held to that high bar.

The High Bar

In these organizations, the leaders are driving toward a high bar of excellence. Here are actual quotes from leadership in these organizations that demonstrate a different way of thinking.

- "The best and fastest way to deliver a high-quality product to our customers is to put a high-quality product into testing. Give me your plan to achieve that."
- "Your current schedule plan is meaningless without a plan for quality. I need to see quality metrics."
- "I expect everyone in this organization to become masters of their crafts."
- "Get Hank and his teammates training in this new technology area. We are seeing indicators of quality issues we have to remedy now."

This is indeed a different mindset. These leaders understand that excellence is a critical business enabler. For example, in developing high-technology software products, these leaders know that high quality belongs to developers and that high quality actually results in faster time to market and higher customer delight.

There is something more. They also know that in spite of any whining that may occur initially, in the end people are proud of producing great products and great results. People crave the high bar of excellence. These leaders are fearless in setting that high bar.

Know that excellence is achievable. Be courageous and set the bar of excellence high. Provide the investment and belief in your people that they can learn how. The results will amaze your organization and your customers.

• KEY #5 •

Understand the Power of Gelled Teams

Here is the secret role of exceptional leadership.

Your role is not to get things done, although you are absolutely accountable when things don't get done. Your role is actually not to get things done through others either, although that is how most leaders start.

The real role of exceptional leadership is to create a culture where people do extraordinary things! One of the best ways to do this is to understand the power of gelled teams.

Jennifer was leading a team on a high-pressure project. The team had been together for a few years, so they had been through many projects like this before. However, Jennifer was the new team leader, and she had done things differently. She set expectations high. She gave the team direction but her constant focus was on creating a team that owned their process, their plans, and their results.

One day, two of the team members came into her office and shut the door. They said "Dan is going to be a problem again. He was a problem in the last two projects, and his way of working and his quality caused both to have very bad results. We went to the manager we had then and he did nothing to fix the problem. We know you are different. Can you help?"

Jennifer looked at them and paused for a long moment and then said "Whose problem is this?" She then waited patiently as their looks went from confusion to understanding. The team members said "You are saying that it is a team problem, our problem. You are saying we need to go talk to Dan. We need to work it out."

Jennifer said, "You said it well. And yes, that is what I mean. Do you need any guidance in how to talk to Dan?"

The team members were worried about taking ownership of the problem, but because of the way Jennifer had been forming the team culture, they really did understand that it was up to them and the team to make the necessary improvements. They listened to Jennifer's guidance and then talked to Dan. It turned out that Dan was very thankful for them coming to him. Dan was lost on some key parts of the technology and had been afraid to come to anyone for help. The whole team rallied together and helped Dan become a great contributor to the overall project.

In discussing this with Jennifer, I found it amazing that Jennifer knew about the problem with Dan and was waiting for the opportunity to get the rest of the team to tackle it. She knew that it would further bond the team and strengthen their ownership of the mission. She was right. The team energy and commitment grew throughout the project.

Once you have created your first gelled team, you will work continually to find more ways to create gelled teams and improve how you do so. After creating gelled teams that you lead, as an executive you will work to create a culture of leadership where that is the norm.

When there are people problems in the organization like those described in the taxonomy of difficult people, many leaders understand that it is their responsibility to ensure that the trouble is fixed. However, many miss the point that they do not have to do it themselves.

The exceptional leader is always looking for ways to create teams of people in which the team can figure out how to address the trouble without management involvement. As you grow as a leader, the troubles you and your organization encounter will not diminish, but as your skills grow at creating the desired culture, the number of times you must personally get involved will greatly diminish.

• KEY #6 •

Treat Trouble as Information-Rich Data

You are holding a meeting with your team. One individual is on an especially long cynical diatribe and is enabling many others to join the conversation.

What is your reaction?

You are the executive responsible for multiple projects where almost all of the teams are missing the deadlines.

What is your reaction?

Your reaction to these types of situations indicates whether you possess the key mindset of treating trouble as information-rich data. The following reactions are sorted from the worst type of reaction to the best reaction.

- The manager joins the diatribe with his own snide remarks.
- The manager begins to argue with the team that everything is really better than they say it is.
- The manager waits very patiently for everyone to finish and then moves on with the rest of the agenda.
- The leader asks everyone to pause for a minute, remove the cynicism, and state more clearly what the problems are.
- The exceptional leader, in addition to asking for clear problem statements, later reflects on why cynicism was the response by the team to the situation. This leader asks what in the environment, including his own leadership, may have contributed to this.

In the second situation, where most projects in an organization are late, leadership responses ranging from the worst type of reaction to the best include the following.

- The executive considers that "situation normal." It is not even thought of as a problem.
- The executive holds critical reviews of all the projects and terminates the employment of the project leaders who were furthest behind.
- The executive looks for pattern differences between the projects that finished on schedule and the projects that finished behind. There is a lessons learned document written and never read.

- The exceptional leader has the lessons learned sessions held publicly and ensures that there is ample incentive for all project leaders to attend. The exceptional leader is looking for everyone to come up with his or her own ideas on how to change the situation.

- The exceptional leader, in addition to ensuring that the lessons learned document is a living document, reflects on how it became situation normal to deliver late. This leader asks what in the environment, including her own leadership, may have contributed to this.

If there is trouble occurring in any of the things you lead, it is important information—not just about the actual incident or the actual trouble, it also contains information on the process, the people involved, the culture you are creating through your leadership, and you.

The best reaction to the trouble is not to ignore it. Nor is it the victim response of whining. The ideal response is to treat the trouble as a rich source of information that can help the organization excel.

• KEY #7 •

Own Your Leadership Power

Have you played racquetball or perhaps squash? In those sports, the two people playing each other are not on opposite sides of a net, like in tennis, they are sharing the same space and hitting the ball toward the same surface. The best players understand that the center of the court is a very valuable space to hold. Rookie players can be easily identified because they consistently are on the edge of the court, never contending for the center.

Even managers with great titles and all the associated responsibilities that come with them have been know to behave like rookie players. They do not take ownership of their own leadership power.

For example, when the manager ignores the cynic and just waits for him to finish, the manager has given the cynic the center of the court. When this is done repeatedly, the cynic becomes the unofficial owner of the meeting. As new topics come up, people will not watch the manager, they will watch the designated cynic. He can kill a topic with a sneer.

The final key to the exceptional leadership power of being able to transform the troublesome to the tremendous is to take ownership of your leadership power. The meaning of this is simply that you understand and own all the keys of the mindset of leading the unleadable.

It means that when you have setbacks in making those mindsets your first response (and there will be setbacks), you don't let the setback become a norm; you forgive yourself and get back on track. It means that you don't let the trouble you have to deal with define your response; you take ownership of your response. You take ownership of your leadership process and the results.

I used to be the rookie on the edge of the court when I played racquetball. When I was playing with one of the best players in the club, he stopped the game we were playing and taught me about the power of the center of the court.

When I actually beat him one year later, he was absolutely delighted. He understood the power of the center of the court so well that he absolutely owned it. He also understood it so well that he insisted on the proper sharing of it.

You should do the same with your leadership power.

REFLECTION POINTS

How would you rate yourself on each of the exceptional leadership mindset keys? Use a scale of 1 (I seldom think that way) to 10 (that is always my first response).

1. Appreciate the diversity of every leaf.

2. Start with the belief that everyone has good intentions.

3. Accept reality but do not let reality define me.

4. Set the high bar for excellence that people desire.

5. Understand the power of gelled teams.

6. Treat trouble as information-rich data.

7. Own your leadership power.

How do you confirm if you are correct in your self-rating?

2

THE LEADER IN ACTION

SPOTTING TROUBLE, DEALING WITH TROUBLE

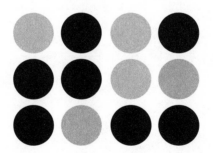

"Action is the foundational key to all success."

PABLO PICASSO

4

Fine-Tune Your Radar for Trouble

I was once leaving a hotel on my way home. I was partially down the hallway and was feeling very happy, which gave me pause. I am often happy, but I was so pleased with myself I asked myself, "Why?" That's when I realized that my suitcase had closed very easily for the first time!

My situational awareness had kicked in.

I immediately went back into the hotel room. I opened the closet. My suit jackets and shirts were still nicely arranged there.

To deal with issues you first must be aware that they exist. And, as in all things, the earlier you are aware of issues emerging the more likely you will prevent damage and achieve the excellence desired.

This chapter is focused on the methods you can use to develop highly tuned radar to catch trouble early.

Before we begin, I have a quick question for you. How good is your radar for trouble? To help you answer this question, consider the following troublesome situations. How often do these types of trouble occur for the areas you are responsible for?

- Quality issues in products found by customers
- Significant issues with quality service to your customers
- Projects that are late
- Members of your teams having significant conflicts
- Teams getting stuck and not making significant progress

The question is not just "How often do these situations occur?" but also "How often do you find out about them well after there was the first indication of trouble?"

Developing a Radar for Trouble

For those who have now objectively determined that their own radars are flawless, scan these areas and see if you find anything new to help make them even better. If you have found that your radar can be improved, consider the following three methods.

METHOD #1
Talk to people. More importantly, listen to people.

The most obvious way to be able to spot trouble is to be there when the situation is beginning or at least right when it happens. And since you cannot always be there, the next most obvious way is to hear about troublesome situations soon after they happen.

One way to do this is by the classic "management by walking around" or, in this very connected world filled with distributed teams, leadership by calling around and checking in. You have two goals with this. The first goal is to find out if there are any situations that need your help to ensure the achievement of the project goals. The second goal is even more important. That goal is to build trust in a way that people will come to you without fear about difficult situations.

The way you conduct yourself in listening and in responding will build the foundation of trust. Thus, the leader must provide help that is actually helpful, as opposed to "anti-help," which many people feel they actually receive when they raise issues, such as being forced into endless fact finding and status reporting instead of actually attacking the root causes.

The following are the keys to making your walkabouts successful.

- Ask questions about the project and the person.
- Vary the questions you ask. The most boring meetings are the ones that ask the same questions of each person week after week. The status in these meetings is often abbreviated to NNTR (nothing new to report). This same thing can happen on walkabouts.
- Make sure you are in the right mindset before doing a walkabout. If you are stressed or distracted, your walkabout could do more harm than good. So set your troubles aside. Make room for their troubles.
- Listen. Listen. Listen. The biggest mistake leaders make on walkabouts is listening to the first part of a problem and, before the speaker is finished, jumping in with advice or solutions.
- Wait for people to finish—even if the solution is obvious to you! If you can't wait because of time pressures on you, let the person know that. Instead of just cutting them off, ask them to provide you a concise summary on the spot. Too often, people try to provide a

long background story before getting to what the key problem is. Simply say, "Tell me the core problem or question. If I need more background, I will ask."

When you do hear about trouble, first ask what the person is doing about it. Then ask for suggestions on how you can help. Of course, use your judgment here. There are situations that are obviously outside the person's control and what he or she is doing about it is telling you. However, much of the time the person is already working on the problem and was just getting ready to tell you when you cut the speaker off with your ideas.

Before offering ideas of what they could do differently, ask if they would like to hear your ideas. This is a good courtesy to give to people. It is also a very useful one. It gives the person who is going to listen a chance to prepare to receive. With that preparation, you are more likely to be heard. Be careful that your suggestions are not criticisms. Just asking questions may lead the person to figure out the best way to handle it. Employees often figure it out after you have walked away and given them time to think.

Follow up. The most important thing you can do is follow up and let people know that you did. By doing these activities consistently and well you become a trusted leader who can be talked to. It makes your radar much better when people come to you at the earliest moments of trouble, well before you would have noticed!

METHOD #2

Pay attention to differences.

Often, the first indicator that something is wrong is a feeling that something is different from previous experiences. The key is to pay attention to that feeling and investigate whether your feeling is meaningful or not. Is there something that needs your attention?

On the surface this sounds easy, but in the turmoil of leading complex organizations, teams, and projects, it is often hard to sort out the significant from the noise in the differences you need to pay attention to.

For example, some differences are so large they will be noticed. If Joe has worn shorts every day of the five years you have known him, it will be very noticeable if you meet him at a coffee shop and he is wearing shined shoes and a suit.

Here are two simple examples of small differences I have seen good managers miss. Joe typically sat at the front end of the conference room table and was now sitting in a chair at the back of the room. Mary always stopped in her manager's office to give quick updates of project status. In the last two weeks, she hadn't stopped in at all.

Joe in a suit might be at a coffee shop before a funeral or he might be going on a job interview. Joe changing seats might be Joe simply wanting a change of perspective or it could be meaningful in that he is actually feeling disenfranchised and removing himself both physically and metaphorically from being part of the leadership.

Talking to Mary, perhaps you find out that she had stopped by but never at the same time that you were there. However, when I have seen this situation it is often because there is a significant issue brewing, either personally or at work.

Notice the differences. Ask about them. The answers could be very interesting.

Many managers are in such a hurry rushing from event to event that they miss these small things that are actually important. In their hurry, they have lost speed. Speed isn't about being in a rush. Speed is about accomplishing things that bring great value. To achieve speed, move quickly in your mission and do so calmly such that you can notice the small differences that have big impact.

Look beyond the first level of data.

Often, project management data says the project is on track. When I examine the detailed data, I frequently find key indicators that the projects would experience trouble later unless underlying issues are addressed quickly. As W. Edwards Deming and many others have said, the key is to "Trust but verify."

People often have a story that goes with data, especially if that data doesn't indicate good news about the project. And although the story gives a great context to the data, the data is still important. If people say the project is fine in spite of what the data says, I find that the data is almost always correct. It is important to go deeper when the story and the data do not match.

When looking at data, the most important thing to do is to ask the following questions.

1. **Is the data providing a compelling answer to useful questions?** For example, the first question being asked in this situation is "Will the project finish on time?" The answer of a yes or no is insufficient. The real question is "When will the project finish and how do you know?" The answer will provide the next level of detail.

2. **Was the data collected accurately and consistently?** What are possible sources of inaccuracy? Can the collection method be cheated? If so, know that the very act of collection is often a disincentive for accurate collection. Using this example, looking at the next level of data you can quickly tell if the predicted

end date is superficial or is based on detailed estimates by all people involved, and get detailed tracking on whether or not tasks were finished completely, well, and on time.

3. **Based on the data, what actions can and should be taken based on trigger points?** For example, to make schedules that can be consistently met, the plan should enable early delivery if things go correctly. Doing this would call for detailed plans to have been built with contingency in them to deal with inevitable surprises. The data tracking should have a built-in indicator that is as useful as a flashing light in the car saying you are about to run out of gas. The associated action (fill it up!) should also be that clear.

Even Radar Has Blind Spots

There are limits to developing your personal radar. If you are a leader of a team of people, even if you still do some work on the team, you are different from the rest of the team and you will be treated differently. In spite of what a nice person you are, team members won't share with you the same concerns or frustrations they will share with other teammates. The higher you go in the organization, the less access you will have to the full story and all of its details.

There are a number of readers thinking right at this moment, "This is not true about me." I know this because I have heard this from every level of leader up to the CEO. The argument I hear is along the lines of "I am not like the others." The clincher for the argument is something like "and just the other week, Sally in development told me the absolute truth about something I needed to hear."

And it was true in that one instance that Sally did tell you the thing you needed to know. However, what you are missing are the other ten things she didn't come to you with because you were too busy, or because she was afraid of the repercussions it would have on her teammates. It also doesn't include all the other people who have never told you things that you or your subordinates really should know.

There are many reasons why leaders are blocked from the whole story even when they have fully developed their radar. I have often found situations where the team members absolutely knew that the trouble was significant yet failed to raise it to anyone in leadership. I always ask why they didn't. It is critical for managers to understand the most common barriers to truth telling.

The Top Fifteen Barriers to Truth Telling

1. Fear of disappointing. People don't like disappointing anyone. To tell the leader bad news would be against how they think and behave at home. They just won't do it.
2. Self-doubt. People have told me that they haven't said anything because "I might be wrong about this. It might not be that bad."
3. Fear of personal or career repercussions. "If I raised this issue, the bad news would stick to me for a long time."
4. Fear of losing future business with clients. "If we delayed the release to fix the real issues, we could lose the customer."
5. Fear of conflict. "They might argue with me!"
6. Denial. "It really isn't that bad."

7. No one else thinks it is a problem. "When no one else has even noticed the problem, it must not really be a problem."

8. Low self-esteem. "I don't believe I am worthy to bring the issue forth. They are too important for me to talk to them about my views."

9. Fear of the issue sticking to the issue-raiser. "If I raise the issue, I am afraid I will get stuck with fixing it—and failing."

10. Low skill in communicating issues. "I just didn't know how to raise the issue. I was stuck on getting the message right."

11. Confusion. "I didn't know who I should tell."

12. Incorrect trust in management. "I thought it was obvious. Management was surely taking care of it."

13. Fear of nothing happening. "I have raised issues in the past and nothing happened. I gave up hope."

14. Not my problem. "They gave us a stupid irrational deadline. It isn't my problem that this project is doomed."

15. Protecting others. "My teammates could get fired over this. I am not taking that on."

Three Methods to Drastically Reduce Your Blind Spots

It is not possible to eliminate the blind spots in your radar completely. The best you can do is to continuously work to reduce your blind spots. No matter how hard you work to do this, there will be some surprise that comes up from an area that was never expected.

The good news is there are three significant ways to reduce blind spots.

Draw from the experiences of others.

You will have a much greater ability to make sense of complex situations when you have a large set of experiences you can draw from. Those who are truly seeking mastery of leadership will grow this experience base by leading many projects, by reading books, and by talking with other leaders about how they handled situations.

You can increase your collection of experiences exponentially by talking with lots of other leaders about the difficult situations they have encountered. The following are the four keys to making these discussions as valuable as possible for everyone involved.

1. **Set the stage for confidential and intimate sharing.** If you truly want to understand how others have dealt with situations, be ready to share one of your own. Also make it clear that anything discussed is confidential. Be clear that your mission is to learn how to better deal with troublesome situations in positive ways.

2. **Ask for details.** Ask when they first noticed there was trouble. Did the leader act right away or delay? Were there earlier clues that they saw? Were there potential clues they missed? How did they deal with the trouble once they decided they needed to act? How did it work?

3. **Question, but avoid judging.** You will hear things that may be against your own personal ways of handling situations. If you find yourself feeling judgmental, it will cloud your listening. It is also likely to be noticed even if it manifests just subtly in your tone of voice or body language. If you notice that you're feeling judgmental and can set it aside happily, do so.

   If the judgmental feeling remains, this may be a good place to explore further with the person. I suggest being open to bringing up your feeling in a way that promotes shared learning. You may say something like this: "I am finding myself troubled about the approach you are discussing. I am not sure exactly why, but it is getting in the way of my learning. Could you tell me more about why you chose that approach and any feelings you have about it?"

I have found that the discussions resulting from this opening of feelings are the most productive of all.

4. **Think about what you learned later and apply your own judgment.** Many people use the same methods over and over again and have them not work over and over again. Yet, they believe they are working. So when you speak to others about their experiences, balance their words by observing the actual results and evidence.

The experiences you collect will help you notice more situations earlier in the process.

METHOD #2

Periodically have an external expert conduct an assessment.

You should periodically call for an external assessment. Properly conducted assessments will provide you with a thorough understanding of complex situations.

Assessments should have a key purpose beyond simply finding out what is going well and not going well. Assessments are much improved when they are focused on an important goal. Those goals could be any of the following types.

1. **Determine the soundness of the project plan.** Is the plan technically feasible? Has the team considered alternative approaches and picked the fastest approach to deliver the most

value to the customer? Has the team made a commitment it will keep or beat?

2. **Evaluate the customer engagement process for developing valuable proposals.** Understand how the customers feel about the process, including long-time customers and prospects that said "no." Work with the team to understand its view of the weaknesses and the strengths of the process.

3. **Evaluate the organizational strategy and how well the implementation plan is working.** Find out how well people understand the strategy without looking at any document. Find out what actions are being done that support the strategy. Find out if actions are being taken that contradict the strategy.

Good assessments will produce reports that have clear and useful guidance for leadership to act upon.

The best assessments will do more than that. The best assessments will result in teams and individuals taking a good hard look at themselves and result in significant improvements created by all those involved. Great assessments fuel the culture of continuous improvement.

METHOD #3

Periodically have an external expert help you collect 360 degree feedback.

Method 2 is an assessment to hold up a reflective, magnifying mirror to the organization. You will learn much from that activity. This method is holding a similar mirror up to yourself with the help of your organization and peers. This is powerful because it will help you learn what the key obstacles are in your quest for exceptional leadership.

This method is very powerful, but some organizations are effectively destroying that very power. These organizations are making 360 degree feedback an institutionalized yearly event on the organizational calendar for everyone. They make it a standard survey. In those organizations, 360 degree feedback is becoming as welcome and useful as "performance reviews." In other words, just another box to fill in at year end.

Even if that is happening in your organization, you can still collect your own 360 degree feedback and restore its power for you. Here are the steps you need to take to get full power from this method.

1. **Get an objective expert to help design and conduct the survey.** This is optional, but the expert will help make each of the following steps more powerful. The remaining steps are written with the assumption that an external expert is guiding the process. However, if you cannot get an external expert, you can substitute yourself in the equation.

2. **Design the survey.** Like the assessment method listed previously, it is very useful to have some specific ideas on the information you would like to collect. Consider a number of categories that would be useful regarding your expertise and your leadership effectiveness. Design questions that you would love to know the answers to. Discuss these with the external expert.

3. **Select a group of people who will provide you with the feedback you need.** The key is to get a balance of peers, leaders above you, and people who follow you. It is also important to think about people you know are fans of your work and those who may be detractors. It is important to have a mix of both. You may be surprised by supporters having issues you were unaware of

and also by the respect that people with whom you have had issues with may have for you.

4. **Have the external expert conduct the written survey.** This can be open-ended questions or a rating system for each question. Either will provide insightful information. The external expert collects and collates this information to be presented back to the leader. Anonymous surveys will provide the most honest information.

5. **Have the external expert conduct the in-person survey.** The external expert can conduct interviews either in one-on-one sessions or in small groups. When the written survey is done first, this enables an in-depth investigation into the areas that you would like more explanation of. So, even if the written survey was anonymous, if there are mysterious results, the follow-up interviews will uncover the more detailed information needed for driving improvement.

6. **Work with the expert to make action items to improve in key areas.** This is the step that many leaders find most useful to work with the external expert on. There is so much information that it can be an overwhelming list. That alone is not a problem; the real problem is that some of the information can be painful to listen to. Many people are aware of their weak points, but hearing about it from others can cloud a leader's judgment in sorting through the results. The expert will help you sort out the most important areas that will be the keystones for your improvement plan.

7. **Plan for improvement.** Chapter 6, "Follow Through: A Bridge to Enduring Improvement," provides detailed guidance on how to do this. The key is to have clearly in mind what things you want to be better at and to let people know that you

are working on it! The other key for this step is to plan a follow-up survey.

8. **Conduct a follow-up survey a few months after the first survey.** Knowing this survey is coming will help keep you focused. It will also help those who gave you the feedback focus on whether or not you are improving. Their feedback will be valuable. The majority of people who have employed this method have exceeded their own expectations regarding how much improvement they achieved.

Spotting trouble is good. Spotting trouble early is better. Develop these methods and more of your own and maybe the unleadable will never get a chance to become that way.

REFLECTION POINTS

1. When leading, what are situations that put you on alert that something could go wrong either with your project or around your project? What previous experiences led you to develop that awareness?

2. Where are your blind spots when leading?

3. What actions have you taken to reduce blind spots?

4. Have you ever taken any actions that have created blind spots?

5

Take Action: Transforming the Troublesome

O nce you spot trouble, how will you deal with it?

The trouble can be a conflict brewing, a conflict in progress, a quality issue, a schedule issue, or any issue that puts the group and mission at risk.

There is a choice to be made by the leader. If action is not taken, it is possible that things just might get better. However, it is more likely that if action is not taken things will get worse, and often in unpredictable ways. It can get worse in big ways, such as larger conflicts or schedule delays. Often, these situations get worse, instead, in small ways, such as a lethargy overtaking the team as team members become apathetic about the mission. If the leader does not care, why should the other people in the organization?

If improper action is taken, it can make things worse faster. For example, consider a leader who suddenly delivers a lengthy monologue at full volume to a troublesome person in a public situation. This leader had waited for things to get better and had let her own anger build until it escaped. This incident led to significant attrition of the team over the next weeks and to those within and outside of that leader's organization to actively avoid her.

It is best to take proper action. To take proper action, proper preparation is required.

This chapter provides the general framework and mindset for working with people who, to put it mildly, are out of compliance with your expectations. The framework is an orderly set of action steps with compassion at its heart.

These steps will help you focus on the person at the center of the trouble and learn how to take action that leads to a positive difference. This framework is effective regardless of the type of situation that arises. You should, however, always use your experience and judgment to adjust to the exact situation with which you are dealing.

The Case of the Team Slacker

When reading the steps for preparation, action, and follow through, consider the following situation that team leader Alison faced.

Alison works for a company located in the northeastern United States that has grown to more than 100,000 employees and has a long history of innovation. Alison aspires to grow her role in the company.

The project Alison was leading was what was known in our organization as a "bright lights project," as it had intense importance to all the executives, including the CEO. The company was counting on it, but there was trouble brewing. The project was getting significantly behind, and the team was blaming Carl.

Carl was showing up late but not very late. He was at all the meetings that he was needed at but didn't seem engaged. These were trouble indicators enough but, in addition, his work was behind schedule and, even worse, it was sloppy.

The pressure and Carl's lack of energy were starting to affect the team. Some members were getting angry. Others were starting to show up late too. The high team energy from project kickoff was fast dissipating.

Alison should have spotted the trouble earlier and acted earlier, but in this situation, she didn't. She realized she needed to act now.

Prepare for Proper Action

As a leader, you have seen situations where it was clear that if issues weren't already apparent, they soon would be apparent to everyone and that they should be addressed quickly. Your ability to handle such situations is greatly amplified if you can first clearly hear your own inner voice. Understand why the situation at hand is important to you and to the group and why it is important that it be resolved.

Mastering this ability to hear and understand your emotions and what is behind them will help you immensely in taking proper action. Four steps are needed to prepare for proper action.

STEP 1

Understand What Emotions You Are Feeling and Why

What emotions are you feeling and why? It is really important to listen to your inner wisdom. If you are frustrated or angry with someone, it is important to stop and ask yourself why. Is the behavior simply annoying or will the behavior negatively impact the organization? Your answers are likely an important part of the discussion you need to have.

Having to deal with situations like the one in the case study is often very upsetting to a leader. There are many reasons why:

- Leaders already have too much to do. Thus, it is upsetting when some unexpected trouble occurs, but more than unexpected, the trouble often feels like it is a pointless, irritating distraction.

- Sometimes it seems that the greater the pressure the project and the leader are under, the greater the level of difficulty of the situations that arise. Often, it is just that the impact of ordinary trouble escalates if the project is already under pressure.

- Troublesome situations almost always stir up strong emotions. The fog the drama creates makes it more difficult to see the real problems. This is true for the people around the situation and for the leader.

- Confronting people with performance issues is difficult. Talking to people about what they are doing wrong evokes the feeling of being in conflict. Leaders, too, are susceptible to the fight or flight syndrome.

Any of these root causes by themselves can cause upset. When other problems join in, as tends to happen, it can be magnified into a worst-case scenario, adding to the stress level. The typical reactions to these difficult situations are the classics of denial, bargaining, anger, and depression.

For example, Alison had a combination of emotions. She was angry that the project and her own future could be jeopardized if the project failed to deliver on its promises. Further, she felt betrayed by Carl. There was also a feeling of shame that she was letting the overall team down that was counting on her leadership.

Emotions cloak the real problems in a fog that the leader must work to clear away. It takes practice for people to listen to their inner music and learn what their emotions are telling them. Two methods that are useful for this are:

1. **Talk to a trusted peer.** The trusted peer must understand that your goal is to sort out the emotions from the real risks of the situation. A good peer can ask questions and make observations that help you find the core of the issue.

2. **Write down your emotions.** Write down what you see as the root causes of those emotions. Write down likely risks and impacts.

You may have other methods that work well for you. The important thing is to get clear about what the issue is for you.

Alison thought about her emotions after talking to a trusted peer and wrote down the reasons she was angry:

- Carl's teammates felt betrayed and had additional unreasonable stress put on them.
- In spite of her extreme efforts to make a rational plan, and many difficult conversations with upper management, the project was now significantly behind.
- The project was very important to the future of the company.
- She personally felt embarrassed about the situation.
- Carl was causing her to fail her team, her upper management, and the future of the company. Her feelings were amplified because she had experienced a similar situation on a previous team that she had failed to handle.

When Alison wrote down these reasons she was able to separate her emotions from the real problem: Carl was not performing well. The team project was behind and Carl was the center of that problem. She also realized that the situation was not as bad as it felt. This situation could be improved and perhaps completely recovered.

STEP 2
Move Past Negative Judgments and Assumptions

Most of the time we really do not know why individuals behave in problematic ways.

While driving, my wife and I were just starting up a hill with a "no passing" line dividing the road. It was truly a *do not pass* situation. A car going outrageously fast came up from behind and passed us. I was immediately furious at the danger that driver put my family in. I assumed that the driver was evil incarnate. My words reflected my anger. We crested the hill to see the car screeching to a halt in the entry to a hospital's emergency room with medics running toward the car. My assumptions changed and my anger was replaced with embarrassment and empathy.

Why do people act in ways that are disruptive to the team, the project, and the organization? In many work situations, leaders have discovered surprising reasons for the behavior of their troublesome team members. Many times, they learn that the troublesome people did not realize the negative impact they were having on the group.

When talking with a peer or writing things down, work to ascertain what facts and assumptions you have about the situation. The key is to truly realize that many of what you think of as facts are actually assumptions. You most likely do not *know* the reasons the situations are occurring. You may have a hypothesis, and you may even be right. Write your hypothesis down if you have one. However, it is rare in these situations that you really know why.

After Alison had written down the reasons for her anger, she was able to think more clearly. She considered her assumptions about Carl. On reflection, she realized that Carl's past performance was not just good, but excellent. So, she quickly removed "incompetence" and "lack of talent," which were judgments she didn't even realize she was holding in her mind. She did note that it could be a lack of skill in that specific technology in which he was working. However, if it was that, why wasn't he asking for help?

It was at this point that all the judgmental feelings and anger she had toward Carl dissipated. Alison realized she simply had to understand what was going on for Carl.

STEP 3

Prepare Your Clear, Short (Two Minutes or Less), Judgment-Free Message

It is critical to make your message very concise. You want the key message to be heard. You want it to have impact. You want it to lead to positive change. Longer messages always consist of belabored points, emotions rising, and negative judgments creeping in. The person you are working with will then begin to wander in his thinking or interrupt you, and likely start disagreeing.

This is why the two-minute or less rule is critical. Although many people think this is too short, it is actually a bit too long. With practice, most leaders can reduce the clear message to about one minute or less.

If you read the following example feedback out loud you will see that it takes less than thirty seconds to deliver the message.

"Carl, I am concerned. We made a clear plan together and agreed to clear goals and a timeline. I know you are very capable of meeting these goals; however, for the last few weeks you have not met any of your commitments. This project is very important not just to me but also to your teammates and the organization. And your current shortfalls are having a negative impact on your teammates and the rest of the organization.

I am concerned about you. I am concerned about the group. Can you explain what is happening?"

STEP 4

Set Aside Time with the Individual to Focus on This One Topic

It is best that you and the person receiving the feedback meet privately. Do not add other topics to this meeting. It is critical that you focus on your key message.

Also set aside thirty minutes to one hour so that time is there if needed. Most of the feedback sessions I have given, however, have taken less than fifteen minutes with positive outcomes. The time set aside is to give both yourself and those you are talking with the sense that there is plenty of time to work this out.

Alison had her message prepared. She had removed negative judgments. She had time scheduled with Carl. She was ready.

Take Proper Action

Proper action is the center of your lever for change. With preparation on one end and follow through on the other end, proper action is the fulcrum, the critical leverage point to success. This is where you talk with the troublesome person, or even a troublesome group.

Follow these steps when taking proper action:

1. **Meet in a private space.** If necessary, this can be via videoconference or telephone, as is often required in our networked world. However, do *not* use email or other written correspondence, as the most likely outcome is to make the circumstance worse.

2. **Deliver your key message.** Do not start with small talk. Take time so everyone is properly situated, but there is no reason to delay. Delay will make the other person nervous and, even worse, it can make you nervous. You prepared by removing judgment and having clarity about the good the person is doing. Deliver your key concern with respect and empathy toward the other person. Do so concisely and without judgment.

3. **Wait patiently and quietly for a response.** Often you may have to wait a few minutes, or longer, for a response. The key is to be patient and wait for the individual to talk. If you have to wait longer, the response is often an unexpected set of events you did not know about.

4. **Be in the moment.** The best way to prepare for the response is not to anticipate what it will be. Sometimes the response is a complete surprise: a litany of the hard things going on in the person's life. Sometimes the response is quick and easy. Once the response I received was "Alan, I have been falling short of my own standards and yours. I will fix it." Given that you really do not know the response you will get, just be in the moment and listen.

5. **Listen to understand.** Stay focused on what the speaker is saying and how he is saying it. If there are parts you don't understand just keep listening until the person is done speaking.

6. **Reflect.** Tell the person what you heard to make sure you did understand. Reflect both on the facts and the emotions. This is not a place to argue. For example, if the person is saying that you gave him bad guidance, the proper reflection is "You are saying that the guidance I gave you was not helpful. Can you elaborate on that?"

7. **Discuss.** It is fine to ask questions. It is fine to bring up things you are wondering about. The discussion part should not be long. It is just for you to make sure you understand the situation and the other person understands the impact his behavior is having.

8. **Set expectations.** The meeting must provide clarity on what your expectations are. This is the part of the meeting for the other person to listen and understand. Make your expectations clear. Test understanding such that you really do trust that he understands.

9. **Ask for action steps.** It is best if you set up a second meeting for the person to be able to take time to internalize what he heard. He will also have time to build a proper set of actions for moving forward. That is the simplest, minimal action item that should be taken during this meeting. If it went easy and fast, feel free to record the key other actions the person will take to remedy the situation.

10. **Summarize.** Conclude the meeting with a summary.

There are a variety of responses that you would expect when delivering the difficult message that a person is falling short of expectations. You might expect to see anger or rationalizations or many forms of excuses. If you are centered and in the moment, you should focus on listening and also keeping clear in your own mind your expectations of excellence. The concern you started the meeting with was based on those expectations. The meeting should also conclude with that clarity.

The fact is that, overwhelmingly, people do have good intentions and are working to achieve the best results they can. Treating people with love and respect for their inner strength is the greatest part of the feedback you can provide. When you do so, they will most often rise to the challenge and improve the situation.

Alison Takes Action

Alison sat down with Carl. She gave the key message in less than one minute and then asked a question.

The message was simply the fact that the project was behind and the key reason was that the work that Carl had committed to do was not getting done. Alison also noted that Carl was not working in the way she had observed on previous projects. She told him the project needed his top performance, but she was more worried about him than she was about the project.

She asked the question, "It seems to me something has changed. What is going on?"

Her tone was calm and relaxed. Carl reported later to me that she was genuinely concerned about him.

She waited in silence for about five minutes before Carl spoke. With tears he explained that he and his wife had decided to divorce. He was trying to keep it completely separate from his work life, but he saw now that he had failed.

He was then quiet again. After another minute he said, "I have to apologize to the team for my behavior. Also, you know I love this work. I will get back to my prior performance, but I will need help. Can you help?"

Follow Through

After the meeting, Carl walked into a room where the team had just gathered. He apologized and explained his situation. After he and the team talked, the whole team rallied around Carl and offered not just help with work but also various other kinds of support for his unwelcome life transition.

Alison also followed through by talking with Carl's teammates and ensuring that a proper recovery plan was made.

The whole team rallied and delivered a very successful project. Carl's team members looked back to when Carl asked for help as the point of project turnaround. Most of the team members were unaware of Alison's talk with Carl. Carl's act was courageous. He thanked Alison for her courage in being the catalyst for his change and the subsequent success.

Work Toward Mastery of Delivering Feedback That Makes a Positive Difference

A few months after I drafted this chapter and shared it with a client, he decided to use the techniques in a situation he was having. He had an employee who was constantly coming across as angry to all the people who worked for her and around her. My client took a few days to prepare. He had one short talk with the disruptive employee on a Friday and, like magic, the employee had a new positive attitude on the following Monday.

Now months later, my client and the employee are still doing great. The formerly angry employee recently thanked her manager. After the talk she was quite upset but realized first, that her manager was really concerned for her and her future, and, second, that her own attitude problem wasn't about work, but about other things.

She resolved to change her attitude at work and at home. She did. And things at work and home improved.

The first time the team leader employed these actions it took a few days to prepare. With practice he has decreased his preparation time to less than one day. Often he finds he moves through his emotions and past his judgments almost on the spot. Further, the speed of success of the people he provides feedback to is also improving. This is a journey of mastery.

As a leader, it is important to listen to your inner wisdom. If something is upsetting you, it is almost certainly upsetting others. It is a problem to your group. It is your obligation to the greater good of the organization to listen to your inner music and take the actions that lead to a positive difference.

REFLECTION POINTS

Reflect back on times that you received feedback that you needed to improve.

1. What was an example of useful feedback you received that made a positive impact on you?

2. What was an example of feedback you received that was a negative experience and essentially did no good for you, the group, or the leader?

3. What were the essential differences between those two experiences?

4. Repeat these questions for the times you have given feedback both well and poorly. What was the essential difference in how you did it?

6

Follow Through: A Bridge to Enduring Improvement

have participated in various sports activities and follow through was a key to success in all of them. For example, in tennis, as in any racquet sport, the most powerful serve or return occurs when the whole body is properly prepared, moves, and follows through. If follow through is not done correctly, it jars the whole body, and also ruins the shot!

Note that you can have terrible form while serving a tennis ball. You might get an ace. However, without truly proper form and follow through, you will find the ace is just an accident.

Sometimes taking the actions prescribed in the previous chapter does work almost like magic. Things get better immediately and stay better. However, without follow through, you will find them to also be happy accidents.

Leaders must always be prepared for follow through. In many situations, the conversation is the start, and the leader's next step is to help the person to build a bridge to successful improvement. To create a bridge for successful improvement you must start with the following three clear expectations.

The first expectation is to have the intention for successful improvement through collaboration. That intent of success should be one to energize and build trust not just with the individual, but also with the team of people around that individual.

The second expectation is that you as the leader are accountable for the success of the initiative you are undertaking. It is not right for a manager to abdicate responsibility to the Human Resources Department. If it is appropriate in your situation to engage HR officially, please do so because the department will be helpful to work with as a partner, but not when you abandon your authority and responsibility. The best success is achieved when you work directly with the individuals involved.

The third critical expectation is that you start with the belief that success is probable. Chapter 7 details how to make the decision to "remove or improve." This chapter assumes you have chosen the course of action to improve. If that is the choice, start with the belief that improvement is not just possible, but likely.

The Case of the Expert Everyone Wanted to Run Away From

Alison was leading another significant software development project. Hank was a technical genius and responsible for the fundamental architecture and design of the software system. The project started strongly, but now that the team was well into software development, Alison was seeing problems emerging repeatedly. The other software developers were complaining that Hank was going into the system and rewriting their code without ever talking to them. He was also repeatedly sitting with people as they were writing code (without being asked) and telling them what to type.

Besides the other developers getting more upset and less engaged, this behavior was causing Hank to get further and further behind on the work he needed to do. When Alison talked to Hank about this he became agitated and told Alison that without him, these developers would destroy the system. Alison knew from experience that the developers on the project were excellent.

How could Alison get Hank to be a force for good?

The Key Points of Alison's Preparation

Alison took some time to prepare. She talked to many of Hank's teammates. She discussed and reviewed the designs before and after Hank's intervention. It was clear to her that Hank's intervention had led to minimal improvements to most of the designs. There were a couple of exceptions that were important, but they did not discount the trend. Further, she reviewed the project plans in detail. It was clear to Alison that Hank's actions were negatively affecting team progress.

Alison knew that for Hank to improve, he needed much more than a "stop that." He needed to have a compelling "do that" to help him actually remove the negative behavior and work toward a bigger goal. With this in mind, Alison prepared for the feedback session.

Feedback Session

After opening pleasantries, Alison started. "Hank, you are an excellent architect. I have a question. Do you want to be an architect of a few buildings or a thriving city?"

Hank asked, "What do you mean?"

Alison explained. "Hank, currently you are spending much of your time with a few software developers, helping them with their designs and code, sometimes even rewriting. There are two problems here. First, developers are getting very frustrated. The more significant problem is that this project is much bigger than those few buildings you are focused on. Most important, there are more projects that are ready to start. I really need you there. So again, do you want to be an architect of a few buildings or an architect of a thriving city?"

Alison waited while Hank sat pensively for a long moment. "Yes, I see what you mean." Another pause. "But, I don't think those developers are ready. Will those pieces of code, those buildings, be good enough without my guidance?"

Alison listened and thoughtfully responded, "Hank, we can discuss that, but first I want a clear answer. Which would you prefer to be? Take your time to answer. Which would you prefer and why? Convince me that you want that. What would it mean for you? For our projects? Which is more important to you? What would be most valuable for us? Once I know where your real motivation is, we will build a plan to help you achieve that goal."

Hank answered immediately that he would prefer to be an architect of cities and went on to give many reasons why that would be exciting. He also saw opportunities to help improve the productivity of the organization because he saw how improved architecture could improve software reuse and lead more quickly to new product lines.

Alison stopped him after a few minutes with a big smile. "Okay, Hank, I am convinced. I want what you want. Let's stop here and schedule a longer meeting. I would like you to bring to that meeting a few things: first, a summary of your goals and second, a list of the risks that you are worried about if you stop doing your current work on ensuring that these developers do things right. Then we can build a plan together for how to achieve those goals and address the risks."

Alison and Hank agreed to a meeting time. They needed to create a plan for successful follow through.

The Fabric of Successful Follow Through

The properly conducted feedback session puts people on the road to success. Follow through is critical to ensure success. Here are three reasons why.

1. Habits are hard to break. Often, the taxonomies of troubles outlined earlier are habits. The perpetrators may not want to be exhibiting these habits, but because they are habits they often happen. This is especially true in times of stress.

2. Even if the problem is not a habit, there has been a disruption to a previous pattern in the individual and perhaps the group. The intention to improve is the necessary start, but that alone is often insufficient to solve the problem.

3. Success for the individual, the project, and the organization is important. The responsibility of the leader is to the group. Bringing the individual up to the level of expectations of being a positive contributor to the group is your obligation. Thus, follow through is as important as taking the initial action.

The following are some simple yet effective ways to follow up.

Make a Plan

Intentions rarely work without a detailed plan. For example, I have sometimes discovered that people lack competencies needed to do their jobs more effectively. We would then make detailed plans to get them the proper training that would fit their learning styles and objectives.

These troublesome situations have often disrupted the ability to deliver on commitments made by the organization. Plans may have to be refreshed to take into account any corrective actions. It is possible that you may need to have further discussions with other organizational stakeholders or even customers.

Publicly Commit

Have the person make a public commitment to do things differently.

When people expect a behavior and see that it isn't present, they will seek to evoke that behavior. I worked with an executive who often would get upset about various issues to the point of explosive outbursts of anger in public meetings. He was working in secret to *not* have explosions of anger. People who attended his meetings were so used to these outbursts that they got anxious when they didn't occur. Attendees would begin to bring up issues that in the past had caused outbursts. They would do this until he fulfilled their expectations with an angry response.

It was only after he made public his desire to eliminate those outbursts that he was able to make the improvement successful and permanent. His staff was very surprised and humbled to learn that the executive was more upset about his behavior than they were. People shared their own stories with the executive. They agreed to help him. The executive inspired his whole organization with his public commitment to transform this behavior from troublesome to tremendous.

Coach Others on How to Help

A critical factor of success often involves talking with a few of the key people who are involved on a daily or at least weekly basis with the person working on a new behavior pattern. I have coached them on how they can give feedback to the individual that helps lead to the positive difference.

With these things in mind, Alison set out to make a plan for success with Hank.

Plan for Success

A plan for follow through should always focus on a clear vision of where you, the individual, the team, and the organization want to end up.

In Alison's session with Hank, they took less than 90 minutes to create an action plan that made them both confident of success.

Have a Vision of Success

Hank came in with what Alison requested. He had detailed the vision of what his job should be in two or three sentences. Alison and Hank spent fifteen minutes shaping it more until they were both satisfied they could show it to others. The vision statement of success they wrote was:

> *We envision a system architecture that enables high-quality products for our customers and boosts productivity across our division by enabling more product lines with less effort.*
>
> *The system architect will provide the architectural foundation for our division's software product line. This will be done through the following activities:*

- *Providing the overall architectural concept.*
- *Working with lead software designers for consensus on the best approaches that enable global gains without sacrificing specific product line needs.*
- *The system architect will make decisions where consensus cannot be reached in a timely way.*
- *The system architect will provide mentorship of lead software engineers.*

Hank was anxious to talk about his risk list, and Alison listened. Hank did not trust the competency of the development teams to build the software the same way Hank would do it. Alison delayed that discussion. She simply said "I understand the risks you are talking about. I need to think about those. We will come up with actions to address your list. First, let's cover the benefits and indicators of success." Hank agreed.

Benefits of Success

Alison and Hank made a list of the benefits of success, which included the following.

ORGANIZATIONAL BENEFITS

- Remove technical barriers between product lines.
- Enable reuse of software across product lines.
- Enable more developers to understand how each product line works such that people can move between products more easily and be productive in each product line much faster.
- Get products to the marketplace faster.
- Enable significantly more revenue for the organization because of increased productivity of the software teams.

- Enable more revenue streams based on innovations possible from this.

TEAM BENEFITS

- The more people who understand the architecture and the premise behind it, the more autonomy developers will have.
- The developers will feel more ownership of the products and get more gratification from their work.
- It is likely to decrease attrition.
- It is likely to attract more top talent.

PERSONAL BENEFITS FOR HANK

- "I will be an architect of thriving cities."
- "People will not cringe when they see me coming." (Alison did not know that Hank knew this. He did know and he did care.)
- "It will be very good for my career."
- "I will get great satisfaction from seeing others grow in their skill sets." (And he added when he wrote this, "I really need to do less. I shouldn't write the code for them!")

Indicators of Success

Alison then said they needed to answer this question: "What are some things we would see to know if we were both successful?" Hank, being a software engineer, loved this. He started talking about how, for any successful software development project, there must be testable success criteria. He loved this idea.

Their success indicators were the following four ideas.

1. People smile more often than they cringe when they see Hank coming. (Note: This was Hank's idea.)

2. When Hank inspects people's code, most of the time it needs no changes from an architectural perspective. This would indicate that people understood the patterns and accepted them as best practice. Alison actually pushed for a number here and they agreed that 70 percent or more was a good starting number.

3. Hank's design meetings were well attended.

4. Hank and Alison also agreed to do an anonymous meeting survey every six to eight weeks to check on the usefulness and energy-producing levels from the meetings. They want to make sure this was working well.

Follow-Up Actions

Alison and Hank were both excited and tired. It was over seventy-five minutes into the meeting. They quickly wrote down the actions they were going to take.

Hank agreed to talk to the developers and tell them his new plan. Alison agreed to write down all their agreements from the meeting and send them to Hank.

Alison later realized that she made two significant mistakes in the meeting. She should have set up the meeting for longer, or just set up another meeting for later that day so they could finish. They were both so happy they missed two significant things.

First, they did not come back to the risks that Hank was worried about. He was so happy by the end of the meeting he forgot about his concerns, but only for the moment. He was still worried about the competency of his fellow developers and that would be a problem later.

The second problem was interrelated. They did not have a plan to get Hank the support he would need to change his long-time habit.

Neither of these mistakes was an ultimate barrier to success, but it did slow down the success path.

Alison also told me that she realized this was the job she always thought Hank should be doing. However, she had never clearly articulated it in her own mind. She had just let the generic job description be the guide. She had not taken ownership of making her expectations clear. She realized that she should have had this very discussion with Hank long ago. She also realized she had a list of other people she was now going to have this discussion with before there was trouble.

Do Periodic Check-ins

One manager I worked with did a very good job setting expectations with a troublesome employee. In that next week, the employee showed improvement. The manager found himself distracted with other things and did not check in with the employee or the situation until about sixteen weeks later. The situation had decayed to a worse place then it was before. This should not be surprising, as there was absolutely no planning or follow through.

It is important to do periodic checks. These do not have to be long. The most important thing to do in these cases is to focus your check-ins on the new behaviors you are expecting to see. It is important to ask direct questions. If you get an answer of "Things are going well," you must ask for examples that provide evidence of behavior change or lack thereof. The details will provide you with the real information you need.

Alison was very good at doing check-ins. Within two weeks after the Hank planning session, she was checking in with developers who she knew previously had issues with Hank. They were at first not open about the problem. They did not want to disappoint her. When she asked for details of interactions, however, it became clear that Hank had not changed his behavior.

When Alison asked more questions she found that Hank did not really set out his intentions very clearly to other people. He had told them that he was going to be doing more high-level architecture but no more details than that. Much later, Hank confessed that he was so embarrassed about his previous behavior he didn't ask for the help he really needed. He told Alison this when he was thanking her for the next action she took.

Alison talked to Hank and said that she was setting up a meeting with the key developers, Hank, and herself. She wanted to make sure that expectations were set in a way to help achieve the vision they agreed to. The intention was to make sure that the developers Hank had been micromanaging would push back if he fell into previous habitual behaviors. Hank agreed, albeit a bit reluctantly.

Surround People with Support

Alison prepared well for the meeting. It did not take her long. She simply had her questions ready. She was going to follow a pattern similar to the planning session she had with Hank. Alison wanted to make sure that the people in the room were not just listening to what she had to say. Active involvement was required!

Alison could have walked in with some nice visuals and projected them on the wall screen. Or she could have had handouts that represented the vision, the benefits, and the indicators.

It would have been efficient. However, it would not have been effective.

Here are the key steps Alison took with the team.

First, she engaged the team to improve the vision they had drafted. Hank wrote down the elements of his vision on the whiteboard. Alison gave the people in the room three minutes to write down other ideas or questions they had. When Alison went around the room she found a great discussion about the vision. There was excitement about what it could mean for all of them. They naturally started to talk about benefits.

So Alison stopped them and asked them to each take five minutes to write down the key benefits they saw for themselves and for the company. She also asked the team members to write down what they thought the key benefits for Hank were. Alison encouraged people to write things down so they would have the time to really think about things. Also, writing engages a different part of the brain. The resulting conversation was amazing to Alison and even more so to Hank.

The group had a long discussion about the frustrations they were having and how removing them would enable them to grow and learn as developers. It would also remove fear for them of having their work reviewed by Hank.

These feelings could have been perceived negatively by Hank. However, everything was said respectfully with Hank and his goals in mind. And even more important, Alison started on the foundation of benefits for Hank. People wanted to see Hank happier, and they said that he didn't seem happy doing work the way he was currently doing it. They really enjoyed Hank when he was in his space of designing architecture and introducing it to others. This would free him to be where he was most happy. Hank realized they were right. He told me later that he didn't realize how much people actually cared about him.

Hank told the group about his worries and how it is so important that the architecture be implemented correctly. He gave examples where it was not. They had a discussion about that and Hank realized that most of the time it was correct. And when it wasn't correct, the team either asked for help or fixed it themselves.

Hank asked the group to help him know when he was getting too deep into the technical areas that they should own. With much laughter, the group came up with a "warning word" to let Hank know when he was doing the work in a way they didn't want him to be. The safe word was *micromanager*, and that word was actually Hank's suggestion.

Provide Space for Learning New Behaviors

In writing condensed versions of these case studies, it is too easy to make them sound like things were easy. It is too easy to make them sound like there were instant changes.

As noted, this can happen, but change is hard. It is more likely there is an apparent instant change in aspiration. People want to do well. And sometimes they have a remarkably good start.

However, good starts are often followed by stumbles into the previous behavior. These stumbles can be caused by stressful situations, when people often revert to whichever habits were their strongest behavior patterns. Sometimes, people are so used to behavior patterns that the strange new behaviors will make people "poke" them and try to change them in ways that bring back the familiar behavior. Occasionally, someone who had a great focus on the new pattern will go on vacation and somehow get reset and come back to work in the old pattern again.

Hank had a combination of a vacation and coming back to a code review, where he discovered that an engineer had not followed the architectural rules. Hank immediately started to rewrite the design and code for the engineer. He was actually typing the code on the engineer's personal computer! The engineer sat there quietly resenting it but let Hank do it. It was a familiar pattern, and Hank truly thought the engineer was thankful for his intervention.

Later that day, Alison was following up with that engineer and Hank in a meeting on a new feature request. She learned about what had just happened that morning. She called for a ten-minute meeting with just her and the two of them.

The meeting was as short as Alison promised. Alison said she wasn't worried about Hank's mistake. She was worried that he was not going to get the support he needed to achieve his big goals. She knew that people need the space to make mistakes— and also the space to recover. She was focused on ensuring that there was rapid learning and correction. In ten minutes they came up with three actions.

Alison and Hank decided to have a ten-minute check-in with each other at the start of each week for the next four weeks so that they both stayed on track with the new expectations.

Hank said simply, "I made a mistake and I actually noticed! About halfway through I sensed I was off track, but I pushed on. I should have stopped and checked in. I will make sure I do that when I feel things are off."

The engineer apologized. He said "I really should have said the *micromanager* warning word. It just seemed rude." Hank said, "It wouldn't have been. I might have been startled and maybe even initially angry. However, it would not have been about you. I would have been angry at my mistake." The engineer said he would tell his teammates about *his* mistake of not letting Hank know and about their agreement to not let it happen again.

Over the next four weeks, there were some similar mistakes. But they happened significantly less often and were caught when they were occurring. Hank also found himself involved in the start of other projects that truly made him responsible for architecture across connected product lines. He was very gratified that he could now handle the work. In the past, the current project would have consumed him and prevented him from doing the higher-level work required.

Set the Bar High

It is important to set the bar of excellence high. It is a leadership mistake to recognize just effort. It is more important to recognize when success is achieved.

The key to the success of Alison's leadership is that she didn't dwell on the past but kept a positive view on learning with a future focus. In her ten-minute meetings with Hank on Mondays she would ask Hank which of the benefits they agreed to were being realized.

She didn't focus on mistakes. She kept Hank focused on his high bar. This bar of success was mutually created and agreed upon by Alison and Hank. Hank found this extremely motivating, obviously more motivating than hearing every week "Well, you did it wrong, again!"

Also, Alison encouraged Hank to recognize his own success and progress. She reinforced his observations with her own observations and suggestions. She did appreciate his effort, but her main focus was on recognizing not the effort but the achievement.

When her check-ins with engineers revealed that Hank had a flawless week with them as well as being successful with the new engineering projects, she knew it was time for public recognition. She suggested to Hank that they arrange a thank-you lunch with the key developers who helped Hank achieve his success.

It was a powerful recognition of the effort and the journey, but even more important, Hank and Alison had created a bridge to successful improvement.

REFLECTION POINTS

To be successful in helping people transform behaviors from troublesome to terrific, you must follow through. If you are running a race, do not stop at the finish line, run past the finish line. If you are providing feedback to someone who needs improvement, do not stop at the end of the meeting where you set a new goal, follow through!

I have three reflection point questions for this chapter.

1. Can you think of actions Alison could have taken to make this situation worse? Which of those actions have you seen, or done?

2. Do you have any situations you are responsible for currently that require follow up? Are you applying proper actions to that follow up? How do you know?

3. There are times when a leader has to decide between engaging in improvement and engaging in moving people out of the organization. What are the criteria you use to make this judgment?

7

Decision Time:
Remove or Improve?

Your leadership obligation is to the group as a whole. The majority of this book is dedicated to transforming the troublesome to the tremendous. Many of the examples focus on individuals. But do not be misled. The primary purpose that guides your action should have the overall mission of the group in mind.

Consider the case of Hank, the expert everyone wanted to run away from. With Alison's help he was able to recover his trust with his teammates and improve his overall performance as well as that of the team, and make larger contributions to the whole organization. If Hank demonstrated that he was not interested in changing, what would have been the right thing for Alison to do? What if attrition of the group was high and the people leaving said it was because of Hank's behavior? Your actions must change depending on the circumstances to best meet the needs of the mission and your group.

There are circumstances where it is clear that it will not be possible for an individual to improve to the performance level required in the time required. For example, there are situations where only a scant few weeks remain before the launch of a product. If someone is being especially disruptive, it is unlikely there is time to properly remedy the situation when everyone is already under stress. However, even in this situation, you may think that saving the individual is critical for future organization improvement. All the factors involved could make you feel like your head is going in circles regarding what to do.

Unless the troublesome behavior is outright illegal, these decisions are rarely clear and easy to make. Is it the right time to remove or the right time to improve?

Evaluation Criteria for Remove or Improve

All decisions this important must be made in the context of the situation the leader is facing. A number of factors come into consideration. The following are the most important.

1. Has the individual shown the willingness and ability to take critical input and use it for self-improvement? If you do not have past evidence, it does not mean this is not possible, but it is a troublesome indicator. If the person has issues and always indicates that the problem is not with her but with others, then the leader will have a significant challenge.

2. How well liked is the individual by the rest of the organization? Especially consider if this is a fractured group in which some love the troublesome individual while others are ready to quit. These details help determine not just the decision to remove or improve, but also the actions to take in each case.

3. Is the individual able to raise the ability of others through collaboration? Individuals who can bring together a diverse set of abilities and personalities are important assets to organizations. Collaboration skills that are low or negative can negate positive technical skills.

4. Do the technical skills and experience of the individual fit the needs of the project today? Are those skills exemplary or ordinary? The big question is how much impact the removal of this individual will have on the project. Keep in mind that in some cases the removal of an individual means a productivity boost for the group as a whole. This can occur when the person is causing disruptions because of a personality issue or because of poor quality work.

5. Do the skills and experience of the individual fit the needs of future projects? It is important for the exceptional leader to always keep an eye on the horizon. Is it going to be important to nurture these skills for a future project or is this project the last gasp for an older technology?

6. How likely will you be able to acquire the skills this individual has from outside the organization in a timely manner? This is a critical factor. In some markets, many skilled people are readily available. In other job markets this could be a long, difficult search.

The other set of criteria to consider are the choices that you have available to you. Each of these must be considered before acting.

1. You can do nothing and see if the situation corrects itself. This is rarely the best solution but should be carefully considered.

2. You can try to help the person correct the situation within the job the person holds.

3. There can be small modifications to the current job. This is what Alison did with Hank. Note that it was a correction toward what she really needed and what Hank wanted.

4. The person can be moved to a new position or new responsibility in the same project.

5. The person can be moved to a different part of the organization.

6. The person can be removed from the project and the organization.

7. You could hire an external expert to help coach the person to improve.

Using these criteria-based questions and options will help raise the leader above an emotional response to difficult situations, and enable him or her to begin to think clearly about both the situation and the best actions to take.

The Process for Weighing the Options

Taking the criteria and placing them in a table with a rating scale is a quick, visual way to help see the situation clearly. With this, you can look at the past pattern and think about what the future pattern will look like based on your leadership decisions.

The following steps have guided many leaders in these situations. They have helped leaders to arrive quickly at decisions for action plans.

First, for each of the criteria, make a rating in a table like the one that follows. The rating system is based on a scale of -2 to +2.

The negative ratings make it clear when the impact to the group is significantly bad. The 0 in the middle should be used rarely. Typically the 0 indicates lack of information about that specific criterion. Feel free to use a scale that makes the most sense to you.

	-2	-1	0	+1	+2
Ability to take feedback and improve.					
Well loved?					
Collaboration skills.					
Skills and experience versus current needs.					
Skills and experience versus future needs.					
If removed, will it be difficult to acquire the skills we need in the time frame needed? (+2 is very hard, -2 easy)					

Most of the time, you will be able to easily fill out your table. However, if after filling out the table, you have some critical information you are not sure about, you should go do the work to find out what you need to know.

As noted before, the table will not make the decision. You have to make a decision. If you feel stuck on the horns of what the best option is, especially if it is the remove or improve decision, talk to someone who can help. If you work in an organization where you work for other people, get your manager involved. Delegate upward! If you are the CEO, talk to a trusted peer. The trusted person may be able to provide insights that you are missing.

Let's look at an example of improve and one of remove.

Save One to Energize the Whole

Exceptional leaders take people to new levels that they did not know were possible. If faced with a situation where someone is headed in a direction counter to the success of the group, it is also an opportunity to take the whole group to a new level of performance.

When Alison was thinking about the trouble with Hank she filled out my table in her private notebook. It looked like this.

	-2	-1	0	+1	+2
Ability to take feedback and improve.			??		
Well loved?				??	
Collaboration skills.				X	
Skills and experience versus current needs.					X
Skills and experience versus future needs.					X
If removed, will it be difficult to acquire the skills we need in the time frame needed? (+2 is very hard, -2 easy)					X

For Alison doing this was illuminating. Hank's skills were high, and his skills were needed now and in the future. This coupled with his relatively rare skills and experience would make it very hard to replace him. Removing him would be detrimental to the overall project. Alison also knew that doing nothing was not an option.

She also saw that there were two things she really didn't know. She knew that the developers were very frustrated with Hank but no one had quit because of him. Was that a risk? She really didn't know. She also didn't know Hank well enough to know if he could take the input to improve. This clouded her judgment on which action would be most effective. She thought she already knew, but she wanted to find out.

She talked to other leaders who had worked with Hank. She received mixed information about his ability to take input. There were enough people who were very positive that she decided to go into the meeting with the absolute belief that Hank would want to improve.

She had the meeting with Hank and found that he could take input and was willing to try to change. She also had walkabouts to talk with developers that didn't reveal that anyone was upset enough to leave. She decided she had the time to improve the situation and that the group's success really did need Hank's skills.

The decision to go for improvement was obvious.

Sacrifice One to Save the Whole

Sometimes the best decision is to remove. Consider the case of Sanjay and the projects that were in deep trouble.

Sanjay was an executive responsible for multiple business lines. One division had such significant quality and service issues that he was afraid they would result in losing the division's two main customers. That division's business was a break-even venture at best. Losing the number 1 and number 2 customers would not be a fatal stroke, but it would be close. Getting new customers with the current issues was a major concern but, even worse, if the company did get a new major customer, Sanjay believed that it would break the organization.

Sanjay hired me as an expert consultant to help specifically with that division. He felt he had troubles in the other divisions, but this business line was in jeopardy of going out of business without significant action being taken.

We started work on designing an intervention for that specific division. While working, I noticed that he was getting into details that really belonged well below his level of leadership. I asked him why he was getting into that level of detail in this case, unlike the problems in the other divisions where he was very quick to delegate.

Sanjay paused and looked at me thoughtfully. Noticing the long pause, I asked him the hard question. "Will the manager in the troubled division be able to lead them out of trouble?"

Sanjay's answer was a meandering one that could be accurately summarized as "I do not know."

I followed up with another question. "Sanjay, will you ever trust that manager enough to let him run the division? Your attention to this level of detail indicates to me that you don't trust him now."

Sanjay saw the point I was driving toward and said, "I do not trust him now. Most of the troubles in that division should have been prevented by him. Many of the troubles he is having with employees lead back to his lack of tact with the customers and his own employees. I really don't think I could ever trust him to run this division. However, he has been with our company a long time and really knows the business. If you are suggesting firing him, that would be wrong."

I said, "Sanjay, let's stop here and pick this up tomorrow. I want you to think about what your responsibility is. In my opinion, it is to the overall division employees and their customers. Furthermore, you are responsible for all the divisions. Your attention cannot be focused on just the one. You are giving me mixed messages on this executive. For us to be successful, you must be willing to trust this individual and give him the responsibility to improve this division's results."

I asked Sanjay to fill out the evaluation table before we talked again.

The next morning, he brought me the table.

	-2	-1	0	+1	+2
Ability to take feedback and improve.	X				
Well loved?	XXXX			X	
Collaboration skills.		XX			
Skills and experience versus current needs.		X			
Skills and experience versus future needs.		X			
If removed, will it be difficult to acquire the skills we need in the time frame needed? (+2 is very hard, -2 easy)		X			

Sanjay now looked confident, but a bit unhappy and said, "You are right. My responsibility is to each of the divisions and to each of the divisions' customers and employees. Not to any single division and its leader. The right thing is that this leader finds different employment. I am prepared to terminate his employment."

Sanjay explained the table to me. He related multiple occasions when he had asked the manager to change his methods and attitudes. Sanjay was especially vivid about how that manager had been unprofessional with customers who were still mad at him after an incident more than a year ago. When Sanjay asked him to apologize, he refused, saying it was their problem. Based on this and other interactions, Sanjay was convinced the manager could not take feedback and improve.

When Sanjay considered the question if the manager in question was "well loved," he found it was a split decision. Sanjay said there was a small handful of people who did love this manager. Yet many in the group would be happy if he was removed. Sanjay put representative "X" marks in that row to show this split decision.

Sanjay explained that it would not be easy to find the right replacement. However, when he thought about the time frame, he realized that the long-term health of the division was more important than finding a fast replacement. He was ready to terminate the troublesome leader and put an acting manager into position during the search for the new manager.

The questions we must consider are the following: "Did Sanjay make the right decision? Could he have saved the one to energize the whole? Did he have to sacrifice the one to save the whole?"

Sanjay made the hard decision because of these critical factors:

1. The group was on the verge of losing top customers. Those customers did not trust the division's products. There were at least a few who did not trust that manager.
2. There were a number of employees in the group who Sanjay knew would "dance in the aisles" when the manager left.
3. The troublesome leader had not provided any previous evidence that he was willing to improve.

Sanjay knew that he made the right decision especially because the situation was becoming more urgent. Losing a customer seemed very possible, which would likely be an event that could end the business line. Sanjay had to act quickly and needed a person he could trust in the role.

In fact, Sanjay was now upset he had not acted sooner. He had known about this trouble for a long time but admitted he had never had the discussions with the troublesome leader as outlined in this book. The past did not matter; Sanjay had to act in the best interest of the group that existed as it did today.

The change was very disruptive to the group, as expected. However, Sanjay was able to use his decisive move to make it clear that he had a high level of expectation for the entire organization. There were many other actions taken that helped the organization be successful.

The key was that Sanjay made the decision to remove with careful consideration and with the success of the group as a whole in mind. This mindset was the key that led this improvement effort to success.

REFLECTION POINTS

Consider these questions.

1. Review the criteria for "sacrificing the one." Do you have other criteria?

2. Are there times you can remember that you feel you acted too swiftly?

3. Are there times you remember that you did not act swiftly enough?

4. Are there are any situations that you should be following up on now?

3

THE LEADER IN ACTION

PREVENTING TROUBLE

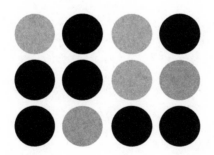

"Prevention is better than cure."

DESIDERIUS ERASMUS

8

The Need for Mountains

was working with an organization to improve its technology development process, which was going too slowly for the CEO. The problem was not that the goals for improvement were too aggressive. It was the constant destructive conflict due to a *clash of the titans.*

Whenever the CEO met with the leaders who worked with him, each meeting was filled with arguments that had repeated themselves many times over. There were passive-aggressive personal attacks in those meetings and in the hallways. Sarcasm was becoming the common way to discuss other leaders and their initiatives.

His biggest frustration was that in the past, this behavior pattern had been rare. The majority of the leadership team was the same group of executives who had stayed with him through much of the journey of the whole organization from start-up to success. They struggled for years simply to survive as a business. During those years, the team members worked hard together to overcome the challenges before them.

His leaders had engaged in conflicts in the past; however, they had always been constructive. They battled about ideas, but in the end they came to agreements that were better than the ones they had before.

In the struggling days of the start-up, they had to work in temporary trailers in a field. The trailers were often way too cold in the winter and way too hot in the summer. They worked long hours.

Now, they were in a real building that the company owned. The company had grown to over 500 people. They started out making customized software for select customers. They now had a product line with multiple customers. They were successful.

Their behavior had changed, and the CEO wasn't sure why. He asked me to help.

The Case of the Clash of the Titans: Finding the Root Cause

To find the root cause, I interviewed each of the leadership team members, including the CEO. I asked each of them three questions:

1. What were three highlights that were personally meaningful to you in the last ten years of the organization?
2. What was the overall goal of the organization in those ten years?
3. What is the overall goal for the next ten years?

The answers to these questions soon formed a pattern. Within a week, I came back to the CEO with the root cause behind the troublesome team dynamics.

Everyone had the same answer to the question "What was the overall goal of the organization in those ten years?" The obvious unifying goal was often stated as a single word: *survival.*

The stories people remembered very fondly from the previous ten years were all about overcoming tremendous obstacles to survive difficult situations. The organization almost ran out of money multiple times. They almost lost key customers multiple times. They had all crammed into hot, badly ventilated, cheap trailers to get the work done in relentless hours of overtime. Together, they had overcome each of those challenges to survive.

There was a very telling thing about the stories of the past. None of the stories that people remembered fondly were about the previous eighteen months. All the stories were from before they had finally achieved economic success. They now had large, steady customers. They had secured significant funding. There had been no recent danger of running out of payroll or of losing customers.

What were the goals for the next ten years? People had wildly different answers. The most common answer was "I don't know."

The root cause of the trouble became clear. In the past, the conflicts were constructive because they were all headed for the same goal of survival. All the decisions had time limits. The conflict was about how to get there. Those conflicts produced positive friction. Then, a decision was made and they moved. Success from each survival instance built trust in each other to face the next survival challenge.

Now the team was without a compelling organizational goal. Coupled with the lack of that compelling goal was that any deadlines the team faced now were not real compared to the adrenaline rush of knowing that unless they did something miraculous, they would run out of money by the end of the month.

The leadership team had run a ten-year journey of survival. They had now crossed a line. They had arrived. However, they were now thirsty for something . . . something more.

The Need for Mountains

In 1914, Sir Ernest Shackleton's Antarctic expedition became shipwrecked. It took 500 days for the commander and his crew to reach safety while living in the harshest conditions our planet has to offer. Years later, though, Shackleton returned to the Antarctic on another expedition, and most of his crew joined him. They went back because they recalled the freezing, starving, dangerous journey as one of the happiest times of their lives. It wasn't just that they relished the challenge, it was that they remembered overcoming the challenge as a team.

There is a need for challenges as high as mountains. There is a need for people to gather together and work toward a great goal. There is a need for quests.

If you see people having the same arguments over and over and again, it is almost always a battle about what the next steps should be, or what the overall solution should be. The root cause of this repetitive argument is *not* about being deadlocked on which solution is superior. If those people battling took time out of the battle to dig deeper they would often find that the individuals deadlocked have different goals in mind. They are headed to different destinations.

Even organizations in the midst of the survival journey are better off if they set compelling goals. For example, Shackleton set a compelling goal before his crew when it was clear how dismal the situation was. Other Antarctic adventures with similar mishaps had resulted in few to no survivors. Everyone on the crew knew this. Before they set out Shackleton set the clear goal. He said with great conviction that everyone would make it back home alive and it was up to everyone to make that come true. After 500 days everyone did indeed make it home. Alive.

Along the way, many of the men kept journals. In spite of the freezing conditions, in spite of the long dark days, in spite of hunger, this was an entry in Dr. Alexander Macklin's diary, which matched many others, "It has been a lovely day, and it is hard to think we are in a frightfully precarious situation."

In some ways, Shackleton had it easy when setting a clear compelling goal. Survival as a goal was obvious. If your organization is successful and survival is a given, the need for compelling goals is even more critical. But how do you set a compelling goal when the obvious one of survival is no longer there?

What do you do as a leader when success, by itself, is not compelling enough?

Seven Ways to Create Compelling Goals

1. **Start with the "big why."** Why is your goal important to you? Even more important, why is it important to your clients? Why is it important to your employees? You can set goals for a period of time, for a project, or to set the stage for creating a new organization. Whatever you set a goal for, start with the big why!

2. **Make your goals about going somewhere inspiring.** Too often, managers put forth goals about "not doing" something. We are going to "stop providing bad service" is not nearly as compelling as "customers will call other people to tell them about the service we provided them."

3. **Be fearless in your challenge.** Outright impossible goals are depressing; however, goals that are outrageously hard and very worth doing are inspiring. Leaders are too often anxious in setting hard goals. They want to make the workplace fun. They may fear attrition or complaining. Fear not. People want to climb the metaphorical mountains that are important. They will invest in the leader who believes they are capable of the difficult journey.

4. **Create goals that are worth the journey.** Goals that are worth the journey are the perfect complement to being fearless about the challenge you set forth. The goal may be difficult. It is possible that we may fail to meet the full extent of the goal. Nonetheless, with great goals, everyone knows it is worth the journey. They know that they will personally be better for it because they were part of the journey. The famous goal to "put a man on the moon by the end of this decade" was hard, was exciting, and to the United States, was worth the journey.

5. **Work on language that will create visceral emotion.** Think about emotions. How can you state your goal so that it will evoke an emotion that people understand, care about, and will remember? Instead of saying, "We need to ensure that we deliver on time" say "We are the exemplars of our industry. Our customers will know that we know more, care more, do more about delivering great value to their needs than anyone else ever can."

6. **Leave room for people to take their own meaning and ownership.** Be ambiguous in details on purpose. If you provide too much detail, it leaves no room for the imagination to take hold. It doesn't leave room for a dialogue. Steve Jobs once told a team that he wanted the "buttons to look so good on the screen

that people would want to lick them." It is visceral, exciting, and worthy. It is also so ambiguous that it leaves room for people to be inventive.

7. **Use your goal to engage in dialogue.** People often complain about ambiguous goals. But that is the secret ingredient to great goal statements. When a goal is put forward and there is no dialogue, there is no way to truly know if it was understood or even heard! When teams engage in the dialogue, even to complain, they will start to figure out what the goal means to them and how they can contribute.

The goals you provide are not the end of the conversation but a compelling start to the conversation. Done in this way, ownership of the goal grows throughout the organization. Further, the results the leader is seeking also grow beyond original aspirations.

Pointing the Battling Leadership Team to a New Challenge

The company I worked with had achieved success. Yet the members of the leadership team were like a sailing ship on a becalmed sea. It seemed that they were not making progress toward anything!

These squabbling, dysfunctional titans did not need a team-building event in the desert. They did not need trust-falls. They did not need training on how to speak politely to each other. They needed a quest that would challenge them intensely. Further, it had to be a quest they believed in.

The CEO worked to create compelling goals that would engage the leadership team and the whole organization in a new quest. The CEO and I worked together to create a speech to set the stage for the next step of his company's journey.

In creating the speech, we worked to follow the hidden structure of many great speeches. That hidden structure is to draw three distinct, inspiring lines for the listener. These three lines represent where we have come, where we are now, and where we need to go. For example, in JFK's famous speeches about putting a man on the moon, he recognizes the past and how very far we have come to reach today. He then goes to the future and draws a compelling vision of where we can go. He returns to the present day and notes the big gap between the current state of the U.S. capacity and how much growth is required to put a man on the moon. He then returns to the past and says we can do it because look what we have done before.

The CEO gathered the entire leadership team at an offsite event and set the stage for what was to come. He said:

> We have come a long way. We remember the various times that we almost went out of business. We remember sweating in the trailers in the farm field we used for offices, putting in long hours across nights and weekends to pull off the impossible.
>
> It was worth it. We have arrived. We are out of danger. Looking backwards we can see that our journey was the hero's journey. We had to battle the equivalent of ogres, trolls, and various other monsters to survive.
>
> We did survive. I am personally relieved to be at a place where we have many loyal customers. We have payroll in the bank well into the future. We have loyal, enthusiastic people working for us. We actually have a real building! We have now arrived.
>
> We are not done. It is time to thrive.
>
> We are not going to be the Chicago Cubs, who last won a World Series in 1908. For our industry we are setting our goals to be

akin to the New York Yankees history in baseball. We are going to from this day forward build our organization to produce multiple championships.

The heroics that got us to this place are amazing. It will take more than that to go to the places that we can go. It is what we learned on that journey that will enable us to do so much more.

I have a set of outrageous goals I am going to lay out for us. They are about our technology, about our industry, about what we can really do for our customers. This workshop we are about to do is to take those goals I have and for us all to wrestle with them. I want us to make them more outrageous. I also want us to create the start of the plan of what we must do to achieve them.

The CEO then went on to lay out his critical three goals about what he wanted this team to achieve in the next five years. He made his goals concise, memorable, visceral, and sufficiently ambiguous. They spoke to the passions of his leadership team and were indeed outrageously hard. The goals pointed to new marketplace segments and also outlined some new product lines that would be extremely hard to create.

After his speech, he had each of the leadership team members take time to speak about the goals including what they would mean to them personally to be able to engage in this quest. He wanted to know how they could make those goals more important, more exciting to the organization and to each of them as leaders. What could they do to contribute?

The ensuing discussion was passionate, exciting, and filled with laughter. I must note that there were some arguments, but the arguments were constructive and built toward a better, clearer, more exciting set of goals.

The CEO gave them a mountain to climb.

It was not the end of conflict for the team. However, it served to transform the conflict from destructive to constructive. The CEO and his leadership team followed through and made sure that transformation was tremendous.

REFLECTION POINTS

Having clear, compelling goals for people to work toward is key to preventing trouble from arising. It is also essential for being able to deal with trouble more effectively when it does arise.

For this chapter's reflection points, I encourage you to engage in the following thought experiments.

1. Do you have any symptoms of trouble that point back to lack of compelling goals?

2. What is the current compelling vision guiding your organization?

3. Is it clear to others?

4. How can you tell?

9

Set Expectations of Excellence

As a leader, you need more than a compelling mission for your organization. If you tolerate sloppy work or bad behaviors, your lack of action normalizes those behaviors.

Exceptional leaders are fearless in setting their expectations of excellence in clear language before and during a project, as well as in the way they handle deviations from the expectations they have set forth. If a leader sets forth an expectation that "Quality is job number one" but has no repercussions when there are constant quality problems, then that expectation is just something written on the wall.

Deviations must be handled with sound judgment, especially when you say that you actually want to go against your definition of good for a specific case. If an organization consistently makes a decision to go against its own definition of good, then one of two things is very wrong: the definition or the ability to judge.

The trick we face then is to be able to set our expectations wisely so we can have a much better chance of getting those true expectations met, or even exceeded. Also, we must ensure that the expectations do not limit leaders in their ability to apply judgment to specific circumstances without undercutting the expectations they have set forth.

The Case of Teams That Are Late with Quality Issues

You may have a friend whom you can always count on to be on time. You may have a friend whom you would be surprised if they were ever early. A division I'll call TopShelf was the always-late kind of friend.

TopShelf was a division of a company located in San Diego, California. It created custom hardware-software applications for clients of the overall company. The division was composed of ten development teams with a total of 400 people.

TopShelf had a compelling vision of where it wanted to go. It knew what it wanted to create. Customers did eventually like and use what was created, but only after multiple problems were solved. Just because the customers liked the product did not mean they were happy with TopShelf management.

Customers were unhappy because they never knew when to expect a delivery and because when they received a delivery they knew that they would be spending at least a few days and sometimes longer sorting out quality problems before they could actually use the software.

TopShelf leadership realized that the company had a significant problem. The leaders saw that all their software development teams were delivering late with quality issues. If it was just one or two teams, it could be a problem with that specific software area, or with that team. However, because it was across the board, leadership knew that it was an issue that had to be solved at the leadership level. Somehow, they were at least part of the cause of the problems.

Leadership of the company needed to work with the leadership of the software teams to transform their mutual ability to deliver great software on time from troublesome to tremendous.

The key thing the executive leadership needed to figure out was how to properly define what guidance to give and what questions to ask to provide the proper expectations of excellence. They wanted to make sure that what they asked for was also what they really wanted and needed.

The TopShelf executives were faced with one of the most frustrating issues listed in the taxonomy of trouble. Yet, they were getting exactly what they were asking for.

The problem was that TopShelf's ability to commit to and deliver high-quality content was dismal.

The leaders realized a very important point. If all teams are delivering well except for one team, the problem is likely within that team. If all teams are delivering inconsistently or poorly, as in this example, the trouble lies within the leadership.

TopShelf was not alone. Many leaders become frustrated by problems their own language creates. TopShelf suffered precisely from that problem. All its managers set expectations for project kickoffs with very similar language. The most common phrases were:

- I want the most aggressive plan you can build. What is the earliest date you can get this done?
- Hurry up and get this to test so we can start finding the defects!

When teams presented their plans, the management often told them that the plans were not aggressive enough, and they asked for earlier dates. The teams said "We will try." When a team makes a plan that truly is "as aggressive as possible," the only possible positive outcome is to deliver exactly on time. The likely outcome is to deliver late—which is what these teams did.

When managers asked about progress, they did not ask questions about quality. They just asked how close the teams were to delivering to test.

The teams did do what they were asked to do. They created what they called "happy plans." If everything went perfectly well and there were no interruptions and no changes needed then they could maybe deliver to that date. They built a plan where they could *never* finish early.

The situation was made worse by the statement about hurrying the product into testing. The team did exactly what the leader asked for and skipped solid development practices and hurried it into test. The testing process took a long time because there were so many defects to find.

Using testing to find and fix problems is the slowest way to build a high-quality product. It is extraordinarily hard to predict how long testing quality will take. The other problem is that testing alone was absolutely insufficient. Quality issues always escaped.

The results were not what they wanted, not what they needed. They were, however, absolutely what they asked for.

The Carpenters Did What Was Asked of Them

TopShelf's problem was very similar to the issues I had with the carpenters I hired many years ago.

My nineteenth-century house had a lot of character and of course required a lot of work as well. During this period I hired a number of carpenters. For some reason, they all were unable to meet the needs I had. All the carpenters had the same issues! This alone was a warning sign that I should have noticed.

They would often start the job and then disappear for days. My house would be in disarray for long periods while I waited for them to finish. I would hurry them up and sometimes that worked, but if I pushed too hard, they finished but left my house a mess that I needed to clean up.

One day I had the sudden realization that the problem was me.

I usually started the initial contracting session with language like this: "I want this job started as soon as possible. When can you start?" Their usual answer was that they could start tomorrow or next week. They were good to their word and did just that.

And the job would take weeks of them stopping in for a few hours here and there.

I realized that the problem was what I was asking for.

I changed my language and questions with the next project with a carpenter whom I had worked with before (and thus had had all those issues with). But this time I said, "I enjoy your company very much, but not the disruption to my house. I want you to start this job when you can be here without interruption. I want the job done well, but in fast contiguous days. Also, do a great quality job. I want the house to be better and cleaner than when you started. This is different from what I asked for before, and this is very important. Can you do this?"

This initially confused that carpenter, and subsequent carpenters and plumbers. They had not heard that language before. However, each subsequent contractor provided me with dates they could accomplish this amazing feat. They all delivered per my expectations. Although the "start date" was much further in the future, the actual work finished faster. Moreover, the disruption to my household was greatly reduced.

I was delighted that I finally figured out that I had been hiring the right contractors all along.

Thoughtful Creation of Expectations of Excellence

Whether you desire to reset expectations or you are forming a new organization or simply a new team, the creation of your expectations of excellence should be done in a thoughtful manner. The following are considerations in forming your expectations of excellence.

Consider the Context of Your Organization

What is the organization's vision and mission? Are you leading a group in a risky new enterprise or is this a critical project building on existing technologies?

What things are most important for your organization to avoid? What are the most important values you want your employees to demonstrate?

For example, I worked closely with an organization whose mission was dedicated to connecting young people to the natural world. Its key interest was setting expectations around the skills and behaviors of the instructors who would be working with young people in outdoor wilderness programs. The results were very different from the times I worked to do this in high-technology development organizations. The outdoor wilderness group focused on personal energy, learning, high ethics, and extraordinary outdoor experiences. The high-tech companies' expectations were focused on collaboration, high quality, and high performance standards related to customers and products.

Take a View from the Outside Looking In

Another important view of your context is to take a virtual step outside your organization and look at it as would your customers and the general public.

For example, looking at Apple from the outside, we know from the company's marketing and actual products what it wants to be known for. It wants to be known for excellent design and high-quality products that work together well in a whole ecosystem. From all the books written about how Apple works, we know that those expectations of excellence are very well defined for the organization. The bar is set high.

What attributes would you like your organization to be known for? Consider what it may be known for right now. Are you happy or is a change needed? TopShelf executives did this exercise, and it was a humbling experience. This was a key driver for them in establishing a new set of expectations of excellence.

Engage Key Opinion Leaders in the Conversation

Whether you are doing this for the first time or trying to inject new energy into what you already have, it is vital to not do this alone. Seek a conversation with people you trust both inside and outside of your organization.

Inside your organization, you want to engage in a conversation that helps form and develop your ideas. Also, by engaging in the conversation you are setting the stage for your key internal opinion leaders to make your expectations of excellence be part of the fabric of how they think as well. They will own those expectations and help them come true.

Engage in conversations with people external to the organization. How do they view your organization now? Do they see you the way you see yourself? Engage them to make your relationship stronger. Also engage them to clarify your thinking and your confidence in what you believe.

Make Your Expectations Concise and Memorable

I was once asked by an organization to help get a project back on track that was very off track. I asked the executive in charge to make his expectations very clear to the team. I quickly found out what part of the problem was. He came into the team meeting and started to show a slide deck of 200 slides of his expectations for the initiative.

The team struggled through the next full day of planning.

I left the meeting, went back to the executive, explained the problem, and suggested that he return and write his top five expectations on the whiteboard. After we discussed this for an hour, he was ready.

He came back and wrote his expectations on the whiteboard. The team discussed those expectations with vigor. After he left the room, the team had multiple breakthroughs and developed a plan of attack that everyone, including the executive, was excited about.

Provide Detail

The slogan "Quality is Job #1" is concise, and in many ways it is memorable. That is important; however, without proper detail behind it, it is unlikely to make any difference. You must provide examples of what *good* is when you say quality is job #1. Leaders should be ready with examples of what they mean by *quality*, especially for the most important aspects of their organizations. They also should have examples of ways that quality can be measured.

TopShelf Defines What Good Means for Their Division

TopShelf's leadership team followed the steps outlined in the previous section. The process was extremely valuable in establishing improved relationships with their customers and with TopShelf team members. No one likes delivering late. The team hated making a low-quality product just as much as the customers hated receiving it.

The work the TopShelf leadership team did was to get everyone aligned on what made good sense for the business and to set the foundation for how to follow up.

The following is a summary of excerpts from the key expectations that now formed the foundation of work everyone was expected to achieve.

"We will delight our customers."

We want our customers to smile when any one of our employees walks into their offices. We expect our customers to know that when they receive a new release of software it will meet their expectations of content and quality.

Everything we do should focus on our customers' experience. When a team is building the plans and designs for the customer, they repeatedly ask themselves, "Will this help the customer with its problems?" When we do designs we ask if this design will help our customers do better work. When we review and test our ideas, we will think about if our customers receive this, will they smile?

"Our focus is on speed to value."

The whole world seems to be focused on going faster. Our speed has a purpose. That purpose is to give the best value we can at the fastest speed possible. When we examine how to pursue our objectives we will work to ensure that they look for the biggest value we can bring our customers. We will look at design alternatives that provide a focus on that value, but further focus on our ability to deliver with speed.

We will look at methods that enable our teams to focus and provide incremental releases with increasing value.

We will use data to ensure we understand where our bottlenecks are and know if we are addressing them. We have more than a need for speed. We have a creed for speed.

"Quality is our top key to speed."

Quality problems lead to customer dissatisfaction. Speed doesn't matter if we crash.

Also, quality problems lead to many of us being engaged in rework. Every time we engage in rework we lower productivity. We will consistently invest in training to develop our abilities in our domain, our methodologies, and our customer needs. We will use data to understand where any of our quality issues are and work to catch them earlier and easier in our process. We do not expect to be able to prevent all defects, but we do expect that we will all work to have a smart focus on quality such that it is a key for us in customer delight and key for us in maintaining our speed to value.

"The dates we provide to our customers are sacred commitments."

Thus, the dates you provide to leadership must be credible! These dates must be commitments to yourself, to me, and, most of all, to our customers.

The message is simple: Make commitments you can keep.

This message does not contradict the need for speed. You must build smart, aggressive plans. Smart plans mean that we have pushed ourselves to look at every possible way to deliver value to our customers as soon as possible.

Once we have made a smart, aggressive approach to delivering value, we are focused on making a smart commitment. A smart commitment means we look at all the risks; we look at our historical data for how long things take. We take into consideration all the other commitments we have already made.

No surprises is a key element of this. Teams need to track their plans closely such that when the inevitable problems arise, they can address them early. If there are going to be problems with making a date, there is early warning.

If we make proper commitments, we should rarely be late. We should often be ready to deliver earlier than the commitment we made.

There are no benefits to delivering late. There are many benefits for delivering early.

TopShelf Transformed

TopShelf executives did two very important things. They began to ask for what they really wanted and needed. They became experts at setting their expectations of excellence. They also gave their teams expert help in raising their skills on both planning and quality practices. They made it clear what *good* would look like and followed up with detailed examples.

Since those changes, the teams have consistently delivered on-time, high-quality releases. Further, the client list for TopShelf has grown significantly.

Regardless of whether the culture matches what is written on the walls, what is important for you as a leader is to be very clear on your own expectations of excellence.

Good managers know what is written on the walls. They might even do a reasonable job of trying to ensure that those things are true.

Exceptional leaders stand out because they will go beyond the stated organizational values and make them their own. The examples provided so far in this chapter are from leaders who worked to get their own expectations clear. The expectations they set were personal. These leaders also ensured that everyone in the organization they were leading knew that those expectations were important.

Set the expectations you want from your organization. If you make it clear that you expect troublesome, you will get it. If you make it clear you expect tremendous, there is no guarantee, but you are much more likely to get tremendous.

The key is to make it personal and make it important.

REFLECTION POINTS

Consider your own expectations of excellence.

1. What are disappointments you have had for whatever it is you are leading?

2. For these disappointments, take a moment and reflect on what role you may have had in setting expectations to get exactly those disappointments.

3. What are your personal expectations of excellence?

4. How do you let people know what your expectations of excellence are?

10

Expecting Excellence Every Day

What happens in the halls and in meetings and many other interactions in the organization define the true expectations of excellence. If those interactions are not congruent with what is written on the walls, the hallways will win. As a result, people will become cynical and leaders will have a more difficult time managing trouble. It is much harder to point to what *good* is with inconsistent reinforcement of the organizational expectations of excellence.

When the formal expectations of excellence match the daily interactions, a powerful foundation is formed that enables the whole organization to rise to expectations of excellence. What is happening is that the leaders are not just creating expectations of excellence, they are consciously forming a culture of excellence that makes the desired behaviors of leaders and team members a natural experience of how they do work. This is the key to preventing trouble from occurring in the first place.

This foundation also makes it much easier to transform trouble to tremendous whenever trouble does occur. Consider the difference when a troublesome person such as the maverick, the cynic, or the diva is the only person behaving poorly in the organization as opposed to being just one of many problematic people. It is much easier to point to that single person as a problem.

As a leader you are much more likely to get what you want if you know what you want and you ask for it. It is most powerful when you have multiple ways and opportunities to reinforce those expectations.

The culture of an organization is formed by a number of common interactions that occur in that organization every week. Which of the following interactions in your organization support or detract from your expectations of excellence?

- ▶ **The formal expectations of excellence.** What is often written on the walls? Do you have a sign on your wall that says "Quality is Job #1"?

- ▶ **How projects are started.** The way in which projects start is a spoiler alert for how projects actually run. Do you ensure that projects start exceptionally well? Or is it more like the way I used to encourage the carpenters to get started, in a hurried messy way?

- ▶ **Project review meetings.** Do the meetings focus on reinforcing your expectations of excellence? Or does the focus neglect nine of your ten items and just focus on one specific trouble area? For example, if quality is your number one priority, but all the questions you ask about are schedule, you are undermining your number one priority.

▶ **Weekly (or even daily) status meetings.** Are the meetings repetitious and dull? Do the topics have a rotation to ensure that all areas of expectations are addressed periodically?

▶ **How meetings are run.** Are the meetings run in the way you want projects to run? Do they start on time and end on time? Are people treated in the way you expect clients and other stakeholders to be treated?

▶ **How bad news is received.** If bad news is always received with anger, it is likely you will not be told bad news as soon as you should be.

▶ **Formal reward and recognition.** What happens when fire starters are rewarded for their heroic firefighting? What criteria are your formal rewards and recognitions based on? Do you find ways to be able to thoughtfully represent the values you want emulated? If your number one value is teamwork, are teams or individuals more likely recognized?

▶ **The training budget.** What does your training budget and process say about your expectations of excellence in regard to the skills you want your group to have? What roadblocks, such as an insufficient budget for classes and too many levels of approvals, have you put in the way of training?

▶ **How easy or hard it is to get the resources you need to do the job.** How hard is it for people to get the tools or other resources needed to do their jobs or improve the performance of the jobs they are doing? In some organizations the process for getting new tools or other resources is a complete mystery. If the process is a mystery, it's less likely anyone will ever ask. This may save expenses, but it is very costly in productivity.

▶ **Project postmortems.** Too many organizations call project postmortems "write-only documents"; that is, someone writes them, but no one reads them. How project postmortems are done and how the results are used can be a key definer of an organizational culture.

▶ **Yearly performance reviews.** Sometimes these are key drivers to how people think about their jobs. Sometimes they are just an annual annoying check-box event that leaders and team members get through as quickly as possible. Yearly performance reviews can be dangerous when given specific results are tied to large bonuses. These are too often tied to one measure at the exclusion of others, which in turn drives the leadership behavior in the wrong direction. How do they work in your organization?

You most likely can make the list longer. The point is if you take the effort to define what good is for your organization, if you define your expectations of excellence, the interactions that happen daily and throughout the year should also reflect those expectations.

This chapter focuses on a few of the key interactions that drive the creation and nurturing of a strong organizational culture.

The Rock and Roll Rhythm That Drives Organizations

Like it or not, meetings set the tone for an organization. If they drone, they can drain the energy from an otherwise good organization. In contrast, if meetings pulse with energy, the potential for greatness grows.

A key part of exceptional leadership is knowing this, taking ownership of it, and working to constantly refresh and improve the drumbeat that drives organizations. Take a moment and consider the following questions.

- How many meetings per month do your regularly attend?
- How many times do you leave meetings feeling energized?
- How often do you feel like you lost a bit of your life and want that time back?

I have conducted surveys similar to this in many organizations, and the percentage of meetings that are labeled as energy draining is depressingly large.

It is not because people do not know how to run meetings. I was once asked to come to an organization to teach a class on how to run meetings. I asked the group of thirty leaders to break into groups of six and provide me with their top recommendations on how to run great meetings. As expected, the leaders did an excellent job and provided the well-known list of best practices for running great meetings.

They knew how. The question was, "Why didn't they do that?" There were many answers, but the solution was simply that they needed to go beyond the basic best practices of sending out agendas, making sure each agenda has a purpose, starting on time, ending on time, etc. They needed to become masters of the rhythm that drove their organization. What follows are the keys to mastering your ability to drive the organizational rock and roll rhythm you desire.

Take Ownership of the Meetings You Own or Run

This may seem obvious, but it is too often not. I once conducted a survey of all meeting attendees on the value of a weekly two-hour meeting that twenty people attended. The survey came back with 100 percent of the people saying the meeting had no value to them, including the chair of the meeting. It turned out they all inherited this meeting from previous leadership and it kept going for two years with no value. It was immediately cancelled.

This may seem like an outlier, but it is not. Many of the people who talk to me about poor meetings are those who own them. They seem to have forgotten they can and should take control.

Introduce Variety into Your Meetings

Vary the rhythm. Many weekly meetings are the same every week. Unless your desired outcome is boredom, vary it. Rotate agenda items. Consider different styles for the weeks. A steady purpose is important, but you can achieve the purpose in many ways. Many leaders doing this build a list of potential meeting topics and styles for those topics. Before each standing meeting they pick which ones are most important to set the pace for that day, that week.

Consider the Types of "Feelings" You Want
Your Meetings to Produce

Do you want your meeting to have a calming effect? Are you looking for the meeting to produce clear action and commitment to those actions for the upcoming week? Do you want to set the stage for breakthrough thinking? Having the forethought to consider this before your meetings and achieving what you set out to represent a truly exceptional difference between good management and great leadership.

Conduct Anonymous Surveys

Periodically, conduct an anonymous survey with questions similar to those provided at the beginning of this section. Find out what people really think.

Work to become a master facilitator. Once you achieve that, keep working toward better. The difference it makes for setting the organizational culture is critical.

Recognize Results, Not Sweat

Fighting fires is admirable, unless you created the fire in the first place. Too often, teams are rewarded for fighting fires that they started. Consider this organization, in which two teams were doing very similar work and leadership wanted to build a culture of delivering great products on time with high quality.

The Firefighting Red Team had followed the old culture of hurrying up and getting their product into the test phase. The test phase was taking a long time because there were so many defects to find. They released to customers, and the customers were calling leadership team members to get the problems addressed and fixed faster.

The Red Team project leader was often before the organizational leadership, giving status updates on how his team members were fixing the problems and the actions they were taking to recover the schedule. The Red Team was working significant extra hours finding and fixing defects. All the Red Team members were extraordinarily proud of how responsive they were. They went in to work early and they left late. They complained about dealing with customer phone calls on weekends, but they complained with pride.

It was obvious to all that the Red Team was working exceptionally hard to delight the customers. You could see the sweat.

Meanwhile, the Green Team project leader encouraged her team members to work differently. They did prototypes they reviewed with customers. They did detailed designs that they inspected in detail for correctness. Team members diligently discussed and reviewed each other's work to ensure the highest quality. Testing of the product found no defects, nor did the customer. This customer also called the organizational leadership. Unlike the other customers, this customer called just once, and it was to say thank you.

The Green Team project leader was only occasionally in front of the organizational leadership team. Her reports were often succinct, with the basic message that everything was on track to an early, successful delivery. The Green Team delivered on time, with extra content, no customer problems, and lots of customer delight.

There were only occasional late nights and weekends. Team members were proactive in talking with the customer about possible issues. They were responsive, but it was not visible unless you watched closely. There was no sweat.

Consider that you are the leader of this organization that had the Red Team, the Green Team, and various other projects. Be aware that there are many project leaders and many team members who are watching your leadership for what defines success in this organization.

As the leader, these are the critical questions that you would face in this situation.

1. Does the Green Team or the Red Team leader have the most name and face recognition among your leadership team? Consider also the overall organization.
2. Which team leader and which team are most likely to be publicly recognized and perhaps rewarded?
3. Which team leader is likely to be promoted?

Unfortunately, in too many organizations the Firefighting Red Team is rewarded and publicly recognized for its great effort, for its sweat. For example, in one organization after the product finally was released to the field, months late, the Red Team was given a big thank-you-for-the-extra-effort party. The Green Team wasn't invited. The Green Team leader in that example soon left to join an organization that recognized her abilities. Meanwhile, the Red Team leader was promoted and encouraged firefighting (and thus, albeit indirectly, fire starting) in all the leaders who reported to him.

In the more rare elite organizations, they reward the results, not the sweat. In those organizations, they hold up the Green Team results as the exemplar that they are shooting for. They hold lessons-learned sessions where the Green Team project leader and key team members present a "how we did it." The Green Team project leader is promoted. The results here are more teams that follow the exemplar model of high-quality, on-time results that delight the customer consistently.

Leaders will continue to practice those behaviors for which they are promoted.

These actions are critical leadership moments that have a great effect on the long-term future of the organization. Consider the organization you want. The key challenge for busy leaders is to be able to see past the sweat and be able to recognize the results.

Use Skills Gaps as Opportunities to Grow the Culture You Need

There are times when you put up the high bar of your expectations of excellence and people simply cannot reach it. The way to keep the bar high is to give people the skills they need to reach it.

First, determine if it is a problem of talent. For talent, I am not referring to skill, but the ability to learn, the ability to excel in the domain the employees have chosen. If you are engaged in improving your organizational culture and find a gap with individuals who were successful before, it is almost certainly not a talent problem.

If it is not a talent problem, it is more likely either a skill or attitude problem. Note, however, that sometimes an attitude problem is masking a skill shortfall because many people are afraid of saying "I don't know how to do that." If it appears to be an attitude problem and you cannot tell if it is a skill shortfall, follow the actions discussed in Part 2 of this book. Often, this will resolve the situation with either an "Okay, I will do this" or the individual being removed from the organization. Sometimes, it results in the confession, "I don't know how to do this"—which brings us back to this section.

In my experience, most of the time it is not an attitude problem or a talent problem. It is simply that people in the organization have not been asked to do work in the way leadership is now urging.

For example, when TopShelf managers put forth their updated expectations of excellence, they really were asking people to work differently. Their first expectation of "delight the customer" was not new. Everyone knew that was the top priority before, and it remained the top goal. That goal was at least partially successful because customers did love the features of the product, even if they didn't like the quality issues or the lack of predictability on commitments made.

TopShelf was now also asking for things that the members of the TopShelf division had not done before. They had not made sufficiently detailed plans to be able to make accurate commitments before. This called for a set of planning methods that no one had undertaken before. Also, the majority of members had only done work where testing was the sole way to develop a product. TopShelf was again asking for new methods to be applied.

To be successful in getting your organization to be successful at meeting your expectations of excellence, you must provide the opportunity of time and resources to learn new skills. This includes various shapes of training and the opportunity to fail—and learn from that failure.

The following are five ways to build skills in your organization to meet the high bar you are setting.

1. Training

Gathering the team and having everyone learn the basics of a planning methodology is often an excellent place to start in skill building. When planning for a training budget and selecting who to give the training to, stay focused on your key purpose. It is not simply acquiring, for example, a course on planning; rather, focus on your culture and the specific success you desire.

2. Coaching

Coaching moves the action from the classroom to the actual work. When organizations are working to acquire new skills, an expert who has achieved the results you are looking for in multiple organizations is the expert you are looking for. The coach needs to be with the people learning the new skills. The more often the coach is there for critical events to provide strong detailed guidance, the more rapid the improvement will be.

The best experts customize all the coaching to be focused on achieving the results within your specific organizational culture. It should not be focused on achieving fidelity to a specific methodology. Too often, leaders are successful in fidelity to a methodology and completely miss the value the project is supposed to be providing.

3. Mentoring

While coaching can be quite labor intensive for the coach, mentoring is where an expert provides occasional guidance. Mentoring is often more focused not on acquiring specific skills but on helping leaders better execute those skills to create the environment, and the culture, they desire. In the TopShelf example, the leadership team had an expert mentor providing the leadership team itself guidance. They also had an expert coach provide foundational training followed by on-the-spot coaching for major events.

4. Clear Role Modeling

TopShelf leaders had to face themselves in the mirror when looking at the organizational performance. As stated before, because all the teams were delivering late, that pointed to the leadership. When the leaders looked closely at the problem, with the mentor's objective help, they saw that they were asking for the wrong thing.

They also saw that they were role modeling the wrong thing. They were consistently late to meetings that they had arranged with their project leaders. They often showed up unprepared and sometimes even asked "Why am I here?" when they had asked for the meeting in the first place.

TopShelf leaders knew that to have their teams perform to their expectations of excellence, they would also have to change.

5. The High Bar, Mistakes, and Learning

The final critical enabler to learning is this trifecta of values. As stated before, if you want learning to occur, you must hold up the high bar of your expectations. This must not relent even when teams are falling short. Do not reward the sweat. Reward the results.

Do not punish falling short. There will be shortfalls, but from each shortfall there will be learning—because you will always encourage learning with key questions about how the individuals and teams will improve with the next iteration.

Gather the Great from the Shrapnel of Failure

Failure hurts.

Let us have no illusions or platitudes around it. If we strive to be exceptional leaders, we will engage in bold projects, and bold projects are not safe. They have risks. There will be failures and they will hurt.

Further, as leaders we will strive to mentor, coach, prod, and encourage those who follow us to excel at the expectations of excellence we have established. Some will fail. It will hurt.

I have not met any leaders who haven't had large, public failures and have not experienced the pain of frustration and sometimes embarrassment of that failure burn through them.

The key action of exceptional leadership when confronted with failure is to gather the great from the shrapnel of failure. The challenge is to use the experience as a learning opportunity for yourself and the whole organization.

Consider the case of a failed project I witnessed, which I call the "Case of the Team Divided." The project team was about 100 people in a very large high-technology company of over 50,000 employees. The team started well with great energy. The team was rich with cultural diversity, and included many of the brightest people in the company. The leadership had given this team the task of building a new paradigm of technology to base future products on.

Unfortunately, the project team had a small schism occur early in the project between two of the strongest technical people on the project. One person preferred a rapid prototyping method he called swashbuckling speed. The other lead technical person was looking to follow a rigorous engineering process. Which was correct? It was never resolved, and the small schism grew into a giant emotional chasm as the project progressed.

The first major technical review failed horribly. The team missed on their promises of what content would be delivered. Further, it didn't work. The anger and finger pointing among the team members was evident in the room with senior managers attending.

They did not disband the team. They used the following steps to bring the team together and as a way for the leader and the team to gather the good from the shrapnel of their failure.

Gather the People

The key for a successful learning event is to set a meeting on the calendar with ample time to work through the key lessons learned. This should incorporate the original idea for the project, the key assumptions the process was based on, the planning process, and the skills and talents of the people working on it. People should properly prepare and be ready to celebrate the learning to take place.

Team members were reminded in writing and at all-hands meetings preparing for the post-mortem about how it would work and what the goal was. There was not any punishment, but there was a high bar set to figure out how to fix it. The team gathered. People were worried, but also optimistic based on the tone the leadership set.

Take a Moment to Recognize and Whine About the Failure

I know Edison said that each lightbulb that didn't work was progress. However, out of those 10,000 "successful" failures, I expect there were at least one or two bulbs flung against the wall in frustration. Whining breaks are an important element of failure!

Start the meeting with time to recognize any of the pain associated with the failure of the project. Make it quick, though—there is real work to do.

The facilitator set the stage for team members to speak personally and specifically about what the failure meant to them. It was not to be a blame session disguised as a whine. It had to be focused on personal experience alone.

The swashbuckling proponent shared how embarrassing the failure was to him and how he felt he had been a contributor to the failure. The rigorous engineering zealot shared a similar story. Many team members contributed to this segment. In a debrief later, attendees commented that this was the key section to the successful recovery. It was not sufficient, but it started the path to success.

Triage the Failure to Find the Great, the Useful, and the Horrible

Hopefully, after the whine break, everyone can put emotions aside. This step is a scientist's view of the failure. I have not yet seen a project where all elements of it were a failure. Triage the elements and find which parts are great, which parts are perhaps useful, and which parts belong on the refuse pile of historical interest only.

The team was able to triage fairly quickly. The group used data to understand which of the technical components were ready for production, which components needed work, and which ones to throw away.

Increase the Value of Your Process

The next step is to reflect on the process used for the creation of the project thus far. See where any holes in the process have contributed to the failure. Seek ways in which you can increase the value of the process, even if that increase in value is finding your way to failure *faster!*

The team members came to the recognition that some of the components required the swashbuckling prototype approach and others needed the engineering approach, and always there was a point were they needed to come together.

The schism was disappearing.

Do Not Make Your Development Process Risk Free

Avoid the critical mistake of trying to make the process risk free. Many processes become large, unwieldy, and so completely safe that the bold has been completely squeezed out. They were so safe they were doomed to fail.

Think of 100+ Ideas You Can Build on the Rubble of Failure

The keystone habit of this action of exceptional leadership must be the ability to generate lots of new ideas based on what you just learned.

The team members walked into the postmortem workshop depressed about the failure and worried about the future.

They left the workshop with over 100 ideas of how to move the project forward and plans for 30 of them to be put into immediate practice. The schism was on the way to disappearing. They were ready for the challenge.

Conducting a postmortem of failures in this way rewards your expectations of excellence. By involving others, you ensure that each person is learning his or her own lessons as well as the lessons from others. If failure is not dealt with in the proper way, it often leads to many of the worst traits from the taxonomy of trouble. Punishing the failure will lead to an abundance of cynicism. Ignoring the failure will make it seem that success and excellence are not important.

Doing a proper postmortem propels your organization forward with style!

REFLECTION POINTS

Consider the list of interactions that strongly affect an organizational culture. They are repeated here for your easy reference.

- The formal expectations of excellence

- How projects are started

- Project review meetings

- Weekly (or even daily) status meetings

- How meetings are run

- How bad news is received

- The questions asked by leadership in the hallways

- Formal reward and recognition

- The training budget

- How easy or hard it is to get the resources you need to do the job

- Project postmortems

- Yearly performance reviews

I encourage you to talk with a peer and discuss the following questions and your answers to them.

1. Which of these factors are the most important influencers in your organization?

2. How do you know? What evidence do you have?

3. What are the interactions happening in those important areas? Are they supporting the expectations of excellence or having the opposite effect?

4. Considering the most important influence points, what actions can you take to help further create the culture of excellence you desire?

11

Exceptional Starts Lead to Exceptional Results

When I was learning the deep strategy game of Go, my mentor told me, "From a good opening, you can lose. However, from a bad opening, you cannot win."

At the time, I thought her little gem of wisdom was just too negative. We can have a great opening and still lose. Okay, that is true. I don't like it, but it is true. I struggled, however, with the thought that "from a bad opening, you cannot win."

On examination of many situations, I found that she was, overall, right. Yes, against a poor player, I could often overcome even a very bad mistake at the start. Playing with good players, it was extremely rare that I could win when I made even minor missteps in the opening. I never recovered from a large mistake.

This is also true when considering how projects or other initiatives start.

Starting a project poorly leads to having to do significant rework later and being constantly behind expectations of schedule and quality. In addition to resulting in constant stress for the project team, projects that start poorly very seldom fully "win" by delivering all expectations on time or early and delighting both team members and customers.

What happens when you start a day waking up behind the planned schedule? Often it results in rushing out to work behind expectations, leaving you almost certainly tired, stressed, and worried about what was forgotten. You hope the day will end better than it started, but it is rare that those days rate high in joy and productivity.

The same is true for a longer period of time, such as a sales quarter. If you start with significant mistakes, such as a horrible transition between customer relationship management tools with incorrect data and angry salespeople, or a problem that's carried over from the previous sales period, it's tough to recover even in three months.

So, my Go mentor encouraged me to take my time at the start of the game to think things through properly. She noted that the best Go players would often spend about two hours on the first 50 moves of the game and spend the remaining two hours on the remaining 200–300 moves of the game.

If you want exceptional results, start toward your goals in the manner you expect to reach them—exceptionally!

The Exceptional Start Challenge— the Problems of Starting Poorly

When a project starts poorly, what problems usually follow?

Think of a few answers and then compare them to the ones I hear regularly in my leadership seminars.

- The project immediately gets behind schedule. This is often true because the team was given a schedule, but even when the team members come up with their own dates, if the project starts poorly they are already behind.

- Stress levels ramp up quickly. This often causes conflicts that take time away from progress.

- Teams are forced to take shortcuts to make some visible progress. This causes the team to have to do significant rework later to fix the problems they created. Often, the later rework costs more than the original start of the project.

- Frequent status updates and requests for recovery plans begin to take up significant time for the leadership of the project and often many other team members, especially the experts. This all takes time out of actually making progress.

- The project and the leadership are almost certain to face credibility issues with others in the organization as well as with the executive team. There will be questions, both about why the team is behind and why the team has a bad attitude.

- On a personal level of leadership and team members, there can be a loss of will. People will start to lose faith that their mission can be accomplished. People will stop asking for what is really needed; they will just show up and do the work. They won't put in the extra thinking required to do it well.

- If there are opportunities elsewhere in the organization or in the general area's labor market, projects that start poorly and don't recover fast enough will face the extra problem of attrition of top talent.

- Projects that start poorly take longer than projects that start exceptionally well. Projects that start well will quickly bypass projects that started earlier, but poorly.

So how do projects start right?

The Exceptional Start Challenge— How to Start Exceptionally

Start by thinking about what you should do. Here, again, are the most effective answers from my seminars.

1. **Have a clear purpose for the project with clear priorities.** Why is this project important to the organization? How urgent is it? Are there limits to effort and cost expense that would make it worthless? It is important to have at least an initial high-level answer to these questions and most likely others as well. Even if the project is an exploration of a possible new marketplace, the project must have a clear purpose defined for the beginning as well as an end result of success in mind.

2. **Understand how important this new project is in respect to the current portfolio of projects.** Is this a tactical urgent response to a current problem? Or is this project intended to be a strategic development to bring new value to an existing or new marketplace? Is this more or less important than current projects?

3. **Choose a project leader whose set skill is commensurate with the project's overall importance to the portfolio of projects.** If this new project is strategically critical and challenging, it is wise to put someone in charge who is ready for the challenge.

4. **Expect leaders to negotiate before the start.** The project sponsor who is funding the project should expect the project leader assigned to his project to negotiate. Their mutual expectations must be explored in a way that they are made very clear, such that the differences that appear will be in sharp contrast. I expect the leader responsible for any project to ensure that the project is starting from a foundation for greatness. If there

is no negotiation, this is a clear indicator that no thought has been put into that very foundation.

5. **Start with a small team.** Too often, projects start with teams that are way too small, and sometimes with teams that are way too big. Typically, starting a project exceptionally means establishing a strong foundation to add other people to later. Starting with a small team with the attitude to start the project correctly will make the project go faster and faster as the right team members are added.

6. **Start with the right leadership sweet spot for the type of project.** Test pilots who love trying out new prototype airplanes are not the perfect candidates for making regular flights between Rochester and New York City. If your project is exploring brand new technology and marketplaces, you want a leader who is fearless about being wrong and learning quickly from taking those risks. If it is a project to build on a current technology for new features or services for a well-established customer base, you are not expecting multiple experiments that could be wrong. You want a leader who will ensure that the current technologies continue to work well for your customer base. Look for the right type of leader for the project context.

7. **Start with a good social mix.** Many people taking part in these exercises have noted when executives assigned people who were known to never get along to start a project. You can start with a volatile mix, but if you are going to start that way, you'd best have a very strong leader who knows how to make the inevitable conflicts consistently constructive. Again, you can start with a volatile mix, but personally I would save adding those ingredients until a bit later in the project.

8. **Time the start to enable momentum to build quickly.** Many of the items on this list are based on the experience of starting up projects poorly. Many times, projects start poorly for the simple reason that no one looked ahead to see obvious conflicts that should have been anticipated. A common example is starting a project two weeks before a long holiday season and having everyone come back after the holidays to find they have to do almost all the start-up work over again. When you are deciding on a specific start date to gather the people, make sure there is ample time and low conflicts for the leadership and the team to start exceptionally.

Do you agree with this list? What items would you change, add, or delete?

Most important, for your organization, how many of your initiatives start with the criteria you believe are needed to start a project to be great?

I have asked this question in multiple workshops, and in every single workshop a mystery has been exposed. The attendees had always created a list very similar to the one I presented here. Yet, their answers were that the vast majority of the projects in their organizations started poorly.

This was hard for me to believe, so I asked the attendees to create a matrix of the criteria they defined and score multiple projects against the criteria. The detailed results showed the truth of their statements. There were occasional projects that scored well on six of the eight criteria listed here; however, the vast majority scored poorly on most of the exceptional start criteria.

There appeared to be a mysterious barrier between the leaders and what they know and what is actually done to start initiatives well.

The Exceptional Start Mystery Explained

We know that we should start projects well. Yet most sponsors of projects fail to do so. Most leaders who are given a project to lead accept the bad start, often without question. Even if they do question it, most eventually just agree to "do their best." We know that if a project starts this way, it will have bad results later. Yet most organizations do this.

Why?

The explanations I have heard from many leaders are very similar.

Explanation #1: We Had the False Understanding That Starting Projects Earlier Would Mean They Finish Earlier

Many people have explained that they believed that starting things earlier meant they would be done earlier. There is truth in that if you start earlier correctly, and then run the project well, the initiative will be more likely to have earlier success.

This belief is dangerous, however, if you believe that it means starting projects as fast as possible, no matter how poorly, means finishing earlier. It does not. Starting early incorrectly will not have the desired effect. As noted previously, it leads to rework, conflict, multiple project delays, and many reasons for the project actually finishing later than if the team waited and started the project correctly.

Explanation #2: The Critical People Needed Were on Other Projects

The second most common reason stated for starting projects poorly was that the leaders did not want to move resources from current projects and initiatives until they were complete. This often led to starting projects with the less busy people—who were usually the people with less experience and skills.

So even if it did many other things correctly, the project still started with a poor base and had subsequent problems, making it difficult to achieve an exceptional finish.

Explanation #3: We Just Had to Get It Started

The third most common reason given for starting poorly after I asked the question "Why did you start if you knew it would be a problem?" was a very honest response. Many leaders have admitted to knowingly starting projects poorly just to get them started. They did so for political reasons to show progress. It was the only way to stop having to give status reports when they were constantly asked "Did you start project X yet?"

If you know how to start projects correctly, and most people do, those are just excuses. They are not the real root causes behind starting projects poorly. The following are the real root causes.

Root Cause of the Excuse List #1:
LOW SELF-CONFIDENCE

Many leaders do not have sufficient self-confidence to say with great assuredness what the right thing to do is. They have irrational doubts such as "Maybe this time, starting early even with the wrong people and with insufficient resources, will have really great results." If they said it out loud that actually would help them!

Root Cause of the Excuse List #2:
FEAR OF UPSETTING PEOPLE

Starting new projects correctly sometimes means that you must take time and money and resources from other projects. This often means either delaying the start until key people are done with existing projects or delaying the new project. Both of these call for making trade-offs and dealing with a number of people who may be very attached to the status quo. Fear of causing this conflict stops many people before they even ask.

Root Cause of the Excuse List #3:
FEAR OF FAILURE

If a new project is worthwhile, it is likely to be a project with risk. There is a possibility of failure. The proposition of a new project is saying "Let's start this new project with benefits that may never come to fruition while upsetting the current projects that might be doing just fine with a bet on the future that we might lose."

There is some reality to those problems. But they can be overcome with the right mindset and with mastery over the proper sequence of steps for an exceptional start.

The Mindset Required for
Starting Projects Exceptionally

Changing the mindset changes the actions taken. The following are the key mindsets to fully acquire that will make starting projects exceptionally natural and as expected. Doing so will make you exceptional among leaders.

A Commitment to Excellent Results

The first critical mindset element is committing yourself to excellence. You may think you do this, but re-examine this. Commit yourself to be part of projects that will have a positive impact, projects that will provide great value to those who are part of them and the customers of the products or services provided. This commitment means that you will consider closely how to start these projects well. This commitment will be true for your thinking if you are a sponsor of the project (you're paying for it!), or the leader of the project, or even a team member of the project. If you have this commitment you will be ready to speak and have your voice be heard!

Consider the TopShelf executive team from the previous chapter. If you asked any of the team members if they were committed to excellence, their answers would have been "of course!" The results betrayed that commitment, however. They had to change not just what they did but how they thought to get the great results they achieved by the end of the chapter.

A Focus on Realistic Expectations

The next critical mindset is to be realistic about the situation. In being realistic, there may be many challenges. Do not let the challenges define your response. Do not let the challenges you face kill the effort before you begin. Face the challenges realistically. Choose to start small with a focus on a simple, powerful value as opposed to starting with all the ideas you have.

No Is a Powerful, Positive Word

Accept in your mind that *no* is a powerful, useful, and actually *positive* word. The lack of ability to say "no" is what drives many projects to start so poorly. The leader did not say "no" to other projects. The leader did not say "no" to starting a project with incorrect expectations or resources. By not saying "no," leaders are saying "yes" to trouble. By saying "no" to other projects to enable a new project to start well, you are saying "yes" to building rapid momentum to success.

Commitment to a Learning Journey of Starting Well

Commit yourself to learning how to start projects well. This whole chapter provides many ideas. I am sure you have many more ideas. Each person's style and situation is different. Develop your own process for starting projects. Be like a scientist and observe the results and adjust your process to achieve better results.

Accept that this is a learning journey, a journey of mastery. On this journey, you shall have bad starts with bad results that are fodder for learning. You shall learn how to say "no" in ways that will make people say "thank you." You will learn the starting process that works best for you. You will learn how to teach others the benefits of the starting game, and how to master it themselves.

Clean Starts Versus Restarts

It is exciting to start projects from scratch. Often, we do not have that opportunity. It is much more likely that leaders are involved with long-term projects or long-term teams, or that they inherit projects already in motion.

Many leaders find it rare to start a project from scratch. It is even rarer that you get to start a brand new project and have that be your sole focus.

Also note that even if your project started well, it is likely there will come a point when the team's plan and also the team itself may begin to deteriorate and even fail. It is not just about starting. It is about keeping it fresh and alive and driving toward an exceptional finish.

Here are some typical examples in which situations may need a restart.

- You inherited a project under way, and it is behind expectations.
- You are given a new project, but it is supposed to use old technology, perhaps even a defective base to build on top of.
- You are given a new project, but you are given it with a customer base that is shrinking while the expectations are to grow the base.
- It is not a new project but one you have been leading and no matter how well it started, there are problems cropping up.
- It is a project you have been leading and it has been going fine, but now you are ready to add forty people to the team and that should be treated as a new start.
- The project is actually going very well, and it is simply time to shift into a higher gear. This too is time for a restart.

Consider, for example, a project that had started exceptionally. The team was doing very well at the two-month point. Team members developed small, usable products, which they tested with a number of ideal customers. Some of the ideas they tested were considered great by the customers, while others drew big yawns. They were also ready to add team members. Meanwhile, outside their control, the marketplace the organization was targeting had added a new competitor. It was time to accelerate the timescale.

The team executed a number of steps to restart the project. Because every situation really is different and calls for your judgment to be applied, you should customize the steps to your situation.

Put dedicated days on the calendar for all the steps that follow. For many organizations, this is harder than actually undertaking the steps. It is difficult for teams in motion to stop and engage in these planning steps again. Nonetheless, this planning is work that must be done. If you watch team sports on television you know that calling a timeout is one of a coach's most strategic methods. Use it!

1. **Have the executive team revisit the goals with the project leadership.** What has changed? Are the goals still valid? What needs to be changed?

2. **Determine whether the leadership of the project is still appropriate.** This is a critical step that is often overlooked. Some leaders, for example, are perfect for the start-up stage and not so good at the detailed work needed to take a product to production. This pause to restart a project is the perfect point to consider this.

3. **Analyze where you have been and where you are.** This is typically a day-long event with some pre-work and post-work. I like to

engage as many of the involved executives, project leaders, and team members as appropriate. What were the accomplishments? What were the disappointments? What is the data telling us? Oh so many questions to go through. Done well, this leads perfectly into the next step.

4. **Do a restart with more detailed planning sessions.** At this point you may have different team members, you may have different goals, and, certainly, if you are more than two months into a project, your short-term plans are either finished or now just wrong. The sessions to make plans will reinvigorate the team and give it a clean start. If the team was behind before, it no longer is. It can now start with a fresh opportunity to win.

The Case of the Problematic Diva Solved by Starting Exceptionally

Josh worked in what I shall call the Bridge the World organization. It is a midsize organization with about 5,000 people. It builds projects for the government that need to be sustainable not just for a few years, but for a few decades. Josh had worked on a number of what was called "team of one" projects in which he created custom solutions as quick wins for the customers. No one knew it yet, but by working in isolation on those projects Josh had become a diva, and he was about to be a problematic one.

The organization was preparing to kick off the Hot Metal project, and the leaders were going to start this one correctly. They had recovered from the "Case of the Team Divided," discussed in Chapter 10. After discussions with me they were ready to try a different method to starting projects as a way to set the stage for excellence and as a way to see trouble early.

Set Project Goals

The members of the executive team spent two hours to put together their goals for the project, both the long-term goals and the goals they had for the initial stage of the project. They were ready to invest in a new product suite, based on new technologies, to provide value to their existing customers in an unprecedented way. They believed that this new product could result in millions of dollars of additional revenue. The executives put together an idea of when they would like the final product ready for market and an initial set of ideas of what the product would do.

However, they did not stop there. They also set out objectives for rapidly building some prototypes so that they could test the premise of their product ideas with customers as quickly as possible. They also wanted the team to discover if they were realistic or unrealistic in their schedule ambition for achieving a full feature set delivered to the customers.

Select Project Leadership

This step was a significant challenge. The leaders examined their existing project portfolio and looked hard at how important this was compared to the existing projects. They forced themselves to rank them by comparing income from the projects for both today and the future, based on projections. They also looked at projected investments to keep the projects alive for the future.

The challenge they faced was that the projects were all important. However, most of the other projects were important tactically. They were to keep today's customers happy. This project was to create a new marketplace and future revenue to replace what they expected would be diminishing revenue in other areas.

They also talked to many of the project leaders and technical experts in their organization. They soon realized that to build the right project leadership team, they would have to take the most experienced team leader from their previous most important project and get her to become part of this project.

They made the hard decision and reassigned her to this new project. They knew that this would have immediate detrimental effects on the existing projects. They planned for this and put supports in place, and they did not do the denial they did in the past that they would have "no negative effect."

Negotiate with the Project Leader

Here is where many projects fail to start properly. Not this time. The executive team expected negotiation and got it! First, the project leader they selected was not happy about the idea of reassignment. She said she would consider it after she studied the project ideas and got some questions answered. She wanted to be absolutely convinced that this project would be set up for success if she accepted the assignment.

The executives wanted and accepted this dialogue. They worked with their Hot Metal team leader to determine the right team members. She wanted a small team of eight people across three of the other leading projects. She was looking for the right technical mix. They asked her to consider the social mix as well, which led to one adjustment. The executives again were ready to take a productivity decline in these other projects in order to get a good start to the new project.

They repeated this socialization process with each team member. They wanted each person to accept the responsibilities for this new project. Note that Josh was part of the team the leader requested, and he happily took the assignment.

The final thing she negotiated or, rather, stated was to make clear that there were no committed dates until her team finished a detailed planning session.

The Detailed Planning Sessions

If you haven't done this in your organization, you really must. This step is the absolute best way to find out what trouble you may encounter on the project later and also figure out ways to prevent it from leaking out in the actual project work.

The leader put her team in a weeklong working session where they had to do multiple things. The executives kicked off the session with their aggressive product goals and marketing goals. The team now had to respond with a realistic plan on how to achieve this. This meant that the team members had to grapple quickly with concepts of what the design of the product would be, what strategy they would use to build the initial iterations, how long it would take, and who would do what work when.

I love these planning sessions because they bring out great emotions, conflicts, and, even better, great ideas. Team members debated multiple ideas, confronted each other with challenges for those ideas, and ultimately tried to settle on a plan for how they would accomplish the goals as well as what they would need from management to do this.

They failed to achieve consensus on an approach for developing the project and how the tasks would be divided. It was a mess, and Josh was in the center of it. Josh wanted everyone to follow the method of developing projects he had been using on his very short "team of one" projects. Even when the rest of the group disagreed, he persisted and persisted loudly.

This was on day 3 of the session. The problem had first appeared on the second day of the planning session. On that day, the team was dividing up key roles by volunteering who would be responsible for the main areas of responsibility for the project. Josh was certain that either he should have the four key leadership roles or that they were not necessary. The team did not allow Josh to do this. Josh relented, but with some anger.

This problem was now back in focus again. A team member complained that Josh was being a diva. Josh said jokingly that he would be happy to play the role of diva.

Josh was starting to get some of the younger team members to gather around him. He was charismatic. Other team members were getting quite angry about the situation. The team leader saw that a schism similar to that of the other project was quickly forming.

The team leader stopped the session and told everyone to take a one-hour break except for Josh. She discussed with Josh the team goals and that this had to be a team project and not a Josh project. Josh kept insisting that everyone else was wrong. The team leader knew that the group was more important than Josh. She did not see any sign from Josh that he would take the "improve" option.

She made the decision that he would not be part of the team but would continue on small projects as a "team of one." The organization did need those projects as well. She asked if he would like to be a consultant on the new project and provide his technical opinions and expertise at the request of the team. Josh wasn't happy about this, but the team leader was firm.

The planning session continued without Josh. The team leader quickly put the Josh issue into the past. She explained her decision and said the most important thing was for this team to be a team. She put them right back to work on making a plan they believed in. The team members jelled around a plan they believed in. Josh actually did provide input, and the team listened to and incorporated many parts of it.

It was important to the Hot Metal team leader to get a reasonable plan. What was more important to her was getting a team that was committed to the plan. The planning session turned out to be a model for how the work would be done. It set the stage for how the team members would work together and showed the limits of what the team leader would allow and not allow.

The team had a fast, exceptional start. If this was a track race, they were off the starting line and running fast.

REFLECTION POINTS

1. How often do you start projects exceptionally? To ensure that you are being realistic with yourself, list the projects you believe started exceptionally. If you want to go deeper, rate how well the project started compared to the eight items listed in the section "The Exceptional Start Challenge—How to Start Exceptionally."

2. What are the barriers for you starting projects exceptionally?

3. What steps will you take to raise your success rate of starting projects exceptionally?

4

LEADING
LEADERS

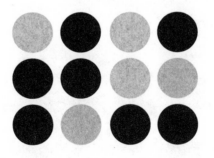

"Leaders live by choice, not by accident."

MARK GORMAN

12

Lead Leaders: Growing Proven Ability

The most fundamental problem of leading leaders is that they can be unleadable too and in whole new ways. As one CEO told me, "The higher up a manager is in the organization, the more fog there is around that manager's performance. It is very hard to judge how well they are doing."

The problem with the fog is it takes longer to see if the leader is the root cause of the problem.

The Case of the New Leader as a Maverick

Sarah was the division leader of a growing $100 million business. Her division employed about 500 people. She hired Tom as one of her leaders after an extensive search to find the right skill set. Tom had lots of ideas that fit what Sarah wanted for the business. She knew that with his ideas and experience he would help take the company to the growth she envisioned.

Over the initial weeks, Sarah noticed significant indicators of trouble.

She noticed that people came out of meetings that Tom ran looking dejected, not excited.

She overheard a loud discussion between Tom and one of the people who worked directly for him. The loudness did not bother her, as she had engaged in many passionate debates herself. The tone seemed wrong, however, and she did not hear anyone else being that loud, just Tom.

She had an instinct that the energy level of her team was getting lower. She could not yet quite articulate why she felt this way, but she knew to listen to her inner wisdom.

Sarah knew that she had to act. The question before her was what specific actions to take and how to take them. Leading leaders is not a lot different from leading individual team members, but there are enough differences that the whole topic deserves special consideration. Sarah became worried that Tom fit the model from the taxonomy of trouble called the maverick.

The Special Challenge of Leading Leaders

Leading a team where everyone works with you personally has many challenges. Typically, the ability to lead people personally and directly will begin to rapidly diminish at X number of people. The X number will vary with the leader, the people, and the situation. I have not personally seen that number exceed thirty people.

Note that I am not talking specifically about how many people are directly reporting to a manager on an organization chart. That situation does apply here; however, I am talking more broadly. For example, there are people with very few others

directly reporting or even none reporting to them on an organization chart. Yet, often these leaders are responsible for initiatives that involve over 1,000 people.

Thus, there are many situations where a leader will be leading
a very large body of people. These people may include individual contributors, team members, and leaders.

In many situations, you may be leading leaders of leaders.

Although there are many similarities between leading leaders
and leading individual contributors, there are significant differences that deserve consideration. The following are the key
differences.

1. **There is increased distance between you and much of the work.**
   Thus, you will often be one or more levels removed from
   where the trouble is and even distant from the indicators of
   trouble. There could be troublesome projects or people who
   could be a risk for your whole organization. The good news
   for you is that the leaders you are leading should take care of
   it without needing your intervention. The question is whether
   they are doing so fast enough. If the leader is not dealing
   with the trouble, or dealing with it incorrectly, how would you
   know? And what actions should you be taking, if any?

2. **You do not know how the work is actually done.** The skills that
   are involved in large initiatives are very diverse. Good leaders
   may actually know the names of even a thousand people
   who work for them. However, they will not know all of their
   backgrounds, nor will they know the details of how the work
   should be done.

3. **Troublesome leaders have a large impact.** If a leader is the one
   creating trouble, the depth and breadth of the impact of
   the trouble grow significantly. The impact of that problem

is amplified in a number of ways. First, it is likely that the trouble is affecting significantly more people than when it is caused by an individual contributor. Second, the impact lasts much longer. A leader always has an impact on the people he leads. The impact lasts longer than the tenure the leader has with those individuals. What lessons have the leader's followers learned? Are those lessons good for the organization?

4. **Your breadth of responsibility increases.** Many good managers find that they are like the legendary vaudeville act of the plate-spinning madman. That person gets plates spinning on a tall stick and then runs from stick to stick to get and keep more and more plates spinning until many crash, with much laughter from the audience. The same happens to many leaders without the laughter around them.

5. **With great power comes great . . . pressure.** The more you are responsible for in leadership, the more intense the pressure most people feel. More and more people are looking for you to make decisions. This includes the people you are leading, the people who sponsor you as a leader, and your peers as well. The impact of these decisions is greater. It is likely that if you are leading leaders, you do feel that pressure. Remember that the leaders you lead also are feeling their own.

6. **There is increased need for autonomy among the people whom you are leading.** This is true when you are "simply" leading team members. It is even greater when you are leading leaders. The more responsibility they have, the more autonomy those leaders require and should have. People need the space and capacity to make their own decisions, to make their own mistakes, and to complete excellent work, with a sense of great personal satisfaction that "I did it all by myself."

Set Your Specific Expectations
for Leadership Excellence

In many organizations, it is obvious to almost anyone when there are troubles in the ranks of leadership. One example of an obvious symptom of trouble is destructive conflict among leaders that leads to conflicts between the teams that they lead. Another symptom often seen is where individuals who work in a matrix organization get different priorities and directions from the different leaders they work with.

In the organizations where there is a significant issue in the leadership, the most common root cause is that the leader of the leaders has not clearly thought about the expectations for how the leaders working for them should lead. If they have thought about those expectations, they are not acting upon those thoughts. Even if there is a strong idea, it has not been clearly articulated. This is the most important preventive measure in ensuring that the leaders you lead will more likely be tremendous than trouble.

Some leaders think that their expectations should be obvious, but unfortunately they are not obvious. There is a great diversity of ways to lead. This is one of the reasons why there are so many books about leadership! Also, within that diversity of ways to lead, exceptional leaders know that different circumstances call for different styles of leadership. The key is to make your expectations of leadership known.

What follows are my personal expectations of leadership excellence. It is fine if you wish to start with my list, but the most effective expectations are those that are specific and personal to you.

1. **Make the noble purpose of the organization your own.** In Lisa McLeod's book *Selling with Noble Purpose*, she shows with stories

and hard data that organizations that clearly articulate not just their purpose, but also purpose that has meaning to the customers, do better in the marketplace. What truly motivates people is typically not money. It is critical for the leaders to engage each other in conversations about the purpose of their organization and of each of the projects that make up their mutual success.

For example, in the medical device industry there is considerable work in the best organizations to ensure that everyone knows that the primary concern is to treat patients expertly and safely with the equipment they create. They are aware that the customers of their systems could very well be themselves or their children.

2. **Take the long view.** As a leader of leaders, you must have a longer view than any of the leaders working for you. The CEOs of larger organizations must be focused on creating next year's business while other leaders focus on delivering today's products, services, and promises. To be clear, I expect everyone to be engaged in thinking about the long-term success of the organization. Each leader must be able to articulate the direction the company is going in and how the success of today contributes to longer-term potential. The ability to provide services to customers is constantly changing in all industries. Besides being focused on satisfying today's customers, leaders must be looking to the distant horizon.

3. **Your job as a leader is to grow the talent of the organization.** John Wooden won a thus far unmatched ten NCAA basketball championships as a coach. Whenever he was asked what was the most important factor, he replied without hesitation, "having the most talented players." Hidden behind that short quote are very important concepts. The first is that you want

to recruit and acquire talent. That is obvious. The more important concept is that it is your job as a leader to grow the talent of each individual whom you lead. It is your job to provide each person you lead with inspiration, guidance, discipline, correction, training, and, most of all, the opportunity to make mistakes and to excel.

4. **Expect the leaders who work for you to challenge you.** If I am making decisions about our direction that you disagree with I would expect you to challenge me. I prefer you challenge me politely and be able to back it with facts. If you can't do that, and you only have an emotional gut feel, I still expect the challenge. Further, if I ask a leader to deliver a project with a key set of attributes by a specific date and that leader doesn't challenge me, that leader has made a commitment.

5. **I do not expect that we will always have harmony.** I expect constructive, collaborative conflict. Each of you who are leaders has significant talent and ambition. I expect each of you to have more ideas than we could possibly accomplish. I expect my leaders to be competing for the rare top talent performer positions in our organization. I do not expect harmony. However, I will not tolerate destructive conflict. We will argue our positions with data, facts, and intuition. I expect that some of the discussions could be loud and emotional. We will stay focused on our common goals. We will make decisions through a process that strengthens our relationships and trust in each other.

6. **Get things done.** You are still responsible for the ultimate success or failure of the overall group and initiative. Is that enough said? As an individual contributor, you are responsible for getting your stuff done. As a leader of individuals, you are responsible for getting stuff done through the

people you lead. As a leader of leaders, you are absolutely still responsible for the success and failure of each of the leaders you are responsible for. I challenge each leader to get things done while growing the talent of his or her teams and collaborating with his or her peers. It is a high bar of excellence. I expect nothing less.

The most critical part is that exceptional leaders know what they expect, and they let the leaders they lead know what those expectations are.

Trouble Spotting: The First 100 Days

Setting clear expectations of leadership excellence clears much of the fog that obscures your view of a leader's performance. This, of course, is not the whole story. The next step is to follow through on those expectations in a way that ensures that your expectations are being met and, better yet, exceeded.

There are two distinct phases of spotting trouble with the leaders you lead. The first phase is when they have just come under your leadership. Many people consider the "first 100 days" to be the most critical. I believe that number varies considerably with the pace and stress of your own organization. The second phase is, naturally, the ongoing work of leadership.

The following are techniques for spotting potential trouble in the first phase of a leader joining your organization.

Ask them to report on the strengths and weaknesses in the organization that they are joining.

When a new leader joins you, I would recommend you set the leader on a mission to interview as many people as is rational in both the team of people they will be leading and across the whole organization. This provides a unique opportunity to do multiple things.

First, you can get a fresh perspective on how the organization is performing. Second, you will be able to quickly judge much of the leader's character and how she thinks about things from the report she provides you. Third, you are providing the new leader a rapid socialization into the organization. Fourth, you are setting the expectation clearly and strongly that you listen to the people she is leading and working with.

I would do this even with people who were already in the organization and are being promoted to new positions. It is perhaps even more important in these situations. They will think they already know about the organization. Taking this listening tour will provide each of them with a whole new perspective. Moreover, people who have been promoted often have a hard time getting other employees to think about them as having this new role in leadership. The listening tour rapidly changes that perspective.

Start the leader with a difficult challenge.

I encourage you to give new leaders difficult immediate challenges with clear sets of expectations and deadlines. I also prefer that they will need more than the team that they are leading and have to collaborate with others within and even external to the organization in order to meet the challenges.

You may consider this "throwing someone in the deep end to see if he can swim." You would be correct. The timing for doing this is perfect at the beginning. Typically, when you bring a new person to work for you as a leader, this is the time when you can provide the most attention to him. The more important thing is that you really do want to know not just if he can swim but how he swims and if there are any troublesome attributes. This approach will help you see any of those troubles and see them early.

Engage them in conversations about the most difficult challenges they are most likely to face while leading in your organization.

If you have been leading the overall organization for any length of time, you will most likely know where the trouble spots are and what issues are almost certain to arise. Provide possible scenarios to new leaders and ask them how they would respond to the situations if they do arise. Provide examples of what has happened in the past.

These conversations are fascinating. You will learn a considerable amount about how these new-to-you leaders think. You will learn about how they are likely to handle situations. Also, your conversations will be active opportunities to model how your working relationships will be. The way you provide guidance here will be a model for how you will provide guidance later.

Each of these techniques helps prevent trouble and identify trouble spots early.

Trouble Spotting: Ongoing Leadership

After the initial new-to-the-organization phase, a pattern for how you work together will be established. As the leader of leaders, you will of course have many things to do. You won't have the time even if you had the desire to be constantly investigating whether your leaders are doing a great job. In fact, you are expecting it.

However, as discussed in Chapter 4, you still want to be continually honing your trouble-shooting radar. All the techniques in that chapter still apply. You want to be able to see trouble coming and be able to deal with it before it is obvious. It is obvious you have trouble when you repeatedly have issues with on-time, quality deliverables. It is obvious when the top talent in the organization is complaining about a leader, and even worse when these talents are fleeing the organization to find better leadership.

Here are a few specific ways to determine whether there is trouble before it has greatly impacted your organization.

The leader's negative attitude days are noticeable.

Consider the impact when one of your leaders is cutting off other leaders or their own team members in conversations. Consider how it reflects on you if a leader you are responsible for is dismissing other people's ideas or concerns with no conversation.

It is amazing to me how many leaders tolerate leaders who work for them and display such negative attitudes. I know there are reasons to be cynical or sarcastic. I know that some days are worse than others. I know that sometimes, one can feel like a victim and just need a minute or two to whine that it is unfair that some negative thing happened.

Do not tolerate this as a daily habit, nor even a weekly habit. If leaders are acting that way with you or in the meetings you are leading, it is likely to be happening even more in situations with the people they lead.

The energy levels of the teams they lead are lower than the rest of the organization.

It is important to watch the energy levels of your leaders and of those whom they lead. As I noted in a previous chapter, it is important to walk around and talk to people. You can also notice the energy levels. Be careful not to react to a single set of events or days but do watch the trends over time. If a set of people seems demoralized, it is almost certain to be that they are, and it is their leader's responsibility to address the situation. Circumstances do not make up the motivation level of the team. It is always the leader.

Engage in a listening campaign.

Ask team members how it is going and then listen. It is surprising to me how many organizations have situations where leaders feel it is inappropriate to walk around and ask about how projects are going. They do not want to undercut their leaders. I understand that, but you are not undercutting anyone if you are giving advice or direction. It is your responsibility to understand how your organization is working. It is actually fine to ask people directly how well a leader is performing. If you have concerns, ask before they are in your office telling you why they are quitting.

Transforming the Maverick into a Positive Power

In the opening of this chapter, Sarah, the division leader, had a problem with her new manager, Tom. Her perception was that Tom was being a negative force in her group, but it was not clear. The following are the actions Sarah took to grow Tom into the leader she needed him to be.

Determining If Her Concerns Were Real

Sarah's experience with Tom was very similar to situations I have helped other managers with. In those instances, I worked with the managers to attempt to remedy situations where top talent was already complaining, with some even leaving when a newly hired manager turned out to be a disruptive force. I say "attempt" because when it is already that late, it is a difficult challenge. Often we have been successful, but never nearly as successful as when catching the problems early.

In Sarah's case, she acted before she had significant problems.

First, she talked privately one on one with her top talent. She stated her observations about meetings and her concern about the energy level of the organization. She did not name Tom as the main source of her concern. She simply asked people whether they noticed anything and if so, what they thought the cause was.

The answers confirmed her fears. Tom was being a maverick for change without any respect for the status quo. Tom had no patience for listening to other people's ideas. He did not show any respect for learning what was good about the existing systems. It seemed all he could see were the problems with how things worked. He was often right but not in a helpful way, not in a way that would build the team. He was instead building resentment toward himself and the organization.

Determining the Root Cause of the Situation

Sarah did not need any other confirmation or evidence to act. She considered letting Tom keep going to see if he would figure it out by himself. She also considered encouraging each of the people with concerns to talk to Tom about their concerns.

Neither of those options satisfied her. The investment her company made to acquire Tom was both time-consuming and expensive. It would be even more expensive to allow the situation to continue just to confirm if her fears were real, or to let Tom figure it out for himself.

She scheduled a private meeting with Tom and prepared her concise, nonjudgmental concerns to discuss with Tom. She noted her observations. She also reported the key points she heard from people she talked to in the organization. She did so without identifying the people.

This meeting led to a lengthy series of discussions between Sarah and Tom throughout the week. They ended up canceling many meetings because they knew they needed to remedy a few problems and they needed a plan to do so.

Building Sarah and Tom's Bridge to Success

The first problem they had to remedy was the broken trust between Sarah and Tom. Tom's initial reaction to Sarah's comments was some denial and some anger. Sarah was deeply concerned about this. She wanted Tom to take the issues seriously and act upon them. She started to lose trust that Tom would do well in the organization. Sarah was focused on building a loyal customer base and creating a great workplace culture. She brought Tom in because of his experience in helping organizations keep pace with a growing customer base. However, this meeting caused her to wonder if he was bringing the strict disciplinary cultures of his previous organizations, which were not known for having great workplace cultures, to her organization.

In their ensuing conversations on this topic, Sarah realized that she had not had a discussion about her expectations of excellence in leadership for her organization. She discovered that

Tom believed that he had been hired as a "turn-around manager." He assumed incorrectly that the organization was failing and that rapid changes needed to be put in place and enforced.

This explained many things. They then discussed Sarah's expectation for Tom, which was to help the company accelerate growth based on the current success. This delighted Tom and led to completely new discussions with great insights from Tom about the stresses that would come with rapid growth.

Tom apologized for how he had been approaching the situation. To rebuild the bridges that Tom had broken, they designed a listening campaign.

The Listening Campaign

The final part of the bridge to Tom's success was the listening campaign. Tom realized that he essentially needed to reboot his relationship with many people in the organization. Tom had not employed the listening campaign at the start of his new role in Sarah's company that I detailed in the previous section in this chapter. Tom did this now.

Tom did report that it initially was not easy for him. He realized that his previous roles were under very different circumstances that called for quick actions. He found that his listening campaign truly changed his perspective on the organization. More important, he found that it established deep trust with those whom he needed to work with to grow the organization.

The most excellent news is they did.

REFLECTION POINTS

The theme of this chapter is growing the ability of leaders. Almost anyone who is in a leadership position has great ambition. There is desire to stretch and grow. Our job as a leader of leaders is to give them the opportunity to do so. It often means staying out of the way and sometimes providing just the right guidance.

In many ways this is the definition of mentorship. This chapter's reflection points focus on mentorship.

1. Think of the most powerful mentor you have had in forging you to be the leader you are today. What was it that made that relationship special so you were able to learn so much?

2. In the mentoring you have done, have you been as good as or better than the best mentors you have worked with? What are the key things you could do to improve your mentoring by an order of magnitude?

3. In what ways could you grow your own skills by mentoring others?

4. If you have managers reporting to you, which ones could use help?

5. What is stopping you?

13

Leader, Lead Thyself: Exceptional Self-Leadership

onsider the stressed, tired, overwhelmed manager. Will she notice the early warning signs of trouble? Will he be able to handle the situations from the taxonomy of trouble in a way that transforms the troublesome to tremendous? How can you handle the maverick, cynic, or diva when you are consistently having a "difficult day" yourself?

It is possible, but it is also unlikely.

If you truly want to be an exceptional leader who can consistently provide great value, to have positive impact, and even to transform troublesome situations to tremendous, then the focus must start with your inner game of leadership.

The following are some of the symptoms of someone who has not yet taken control of his or her own leadership.

Rate yourself on each one of these.

	This Is My Life	Usually	Often	Once in a While	Seldom to Never
Feel overwhelmed by the amount of things not yet done.					
Accept doing things others have asked you to do even though they seem like distractions.					
Apologize for being late to meetings or with things you told others you would do.					
Attend many meetings out of obligation. You get your real work done when you are not in a series of meetings.					
End the week unhappily exhausted.					
Find it difficult to think of work activities that give you more energy back than you put in.					

I have worked with many leaders who identified deeply with this list of symptoms. Many of them were actually very good leaders. Nevertheless, they often felt like they were constantly battling to accomplish what needed to be accomplished.

If you are like these leaders, you rated most of these items as "often" or worse.

The rest of this chapter describes a number of mindsets and methods to take full ownership of your leadership.

Find Your Leadership Sweet Spot

On a tennis racquet there is a miraculous zone known as the sweet spot. If, when swinging your racquet, you miss the sweet spot it will jar your arm, and you are much more likely to miss the spot you are aiming for. Further, missing the sweet spot repeatedly will tire you more quickly.

When you hit that miraculous spot, your body follows through swiftly and smoothly, and the ball is much more likely to spring off your racquet with great speed toward the spot on the court you desire.

The sweet spot on a tennis racquet is where multiple forces are designed to come together to create a harmonic response.

The same is true for leadership. When you do work that misses your leadership sweet spot, it is jarring and more quickly drains your energy. When you do work from your sweet spot, it provides more energy to you than you put into it.

This is also an intersection of three forces that you can control to come together to create a great harmonic response. Let's look at these three elements.

1. **Passion.** This is the type of work that energizes you. You like this style of work and like doing the work in this area. This is the work that puts a smile on your face. You know you are passionate about an area of work when you find that when you are engaged in it time can pass quickly without you noticing.

2. **Competence.** Competence is simply having the skills needed to make the work successful. When you have passion and competence the work done will provide you with great pleasure and pride. You may not necessarily start with the skill level

needed, but if you have the passion it is likely you will acquire it. Further, it is likely you will keep improving.

3. **Value.** To do work that truly energizes you in the long run, the work that intersects with your passion and competence must also be work that provides value to others.

Exceptional leaders are very conscious of what work fits in their sweet spots and what does not. They will work to create ways to grow their sweet spots. They will also try to attract the work they want to do to the center of their leadership "racquets."

When I have mentored leaders to take more control of their own leadership, this is often one of the first things we work on. I ask them to track a week of their activities and to note which activities feel like they are hitting the sweet spot and which activities are jarring. People find this a surprising exercise because they are always learning things about themselves and their work that they didn't know.

Many who have done this exercise learned that there are other factors that affect their sweet spots. Everyone agrees that the three listed are critical. Some people have found other things that are important to them as well, such as the physical work environment, the people they work with, or the financial stability of the organization.

Some discovered that they have more than one sweet spot. They uncover different areas of work where passion, competence, and value intersect.

Many learned that their sweet spots evolved over time. After a period their passions changed and, thus, unlike a tennis racquet, their sweet spot moved!

Most important, they learned that they can make their sweet spots bigger! By taking ownership of their leadership, they guided more work to hit their sweet spots. As they grew better at this, they found ways to also grow their sweet spots through more passion, more competence, and more reciprocal value to those they served.

How to Supercharge Your Energy

Are people more likely to be drawn to a happy, positive leader projecting energy or to an obviously tired and stressed leader?

The answer is quite obvious. Yet, most people act as victims of their own energy levels. So many leaders have told me "I would have gotten more sleep if . . ." or "Those meetings I attend drain me, if only . . ." or "The weeks are so stressful, I am completely drained by the end." The list of excuses for a low energy level is a long and tiring one.

Exceptional leaders are energetic. Certainly, exceptional leaders do get tired. It is not that they are all endowed with a natural gift of infinite energy. The difference is that they have endowed themselves with a very specific gift. This is the gift of finding the best ways of energizing themselves *and* avoiding the things that drain their personal energies.

Consider what happens when we have lower energy, or even feel tired:

- We work slower.
- We get more easily distracted.
- We are more easily stressed.
- We make more mistakes.
- All of which means we work slower on the next day cleaning up those mistakes.
- All of which could lead to not sleeping well and sleeping less.

- Which leads to lower energy, which leads to more stress, which leads to an endlessly exhausting loop.

When people are feeling relaxed and energetic, they typically have a much more productive time. The following things generally result from working from a place of high energy:

- Clear thinking.
- Faster action.
- Fewer mistakes.
- Less rework caused by previous problems created when tired.
- People enjoy being around you.
- You sleep more soundly as there is less stress.

All of which leads to higher energy, which leads to an endless energizing loop.

Anyone who has been on an airplane knows that the flight attendants always encourage the passengers with the standard speech: "In the event of a decompression, an oxygen mask will automatically appear in front of you. If you are traveling with someone who requires assistance, secure your mask first, and then assist the other person."

I have been told by a friend who is a flight attendant that you must do this because once that mask descends there are less than eight seconds before you are unconscious. Putting your oxygen mask on first is a good idea and a good metaphor for a crisis situation.

For daily living, it is more useful to think about your personal fuel management system. Consider your fuel tank, your reserve systems, and how to keep them near full fuel and what to do when you are running low.

It is up to us as individuals to take control of our "fuel management system." Be aware of the energy boosters. Be aware of the energy drains. Be aware of the size of your fuel tank. Take actions to improve. Each investment in improving this system will pay back many times over!

There are four key ways to master ownership of your energy levels:

1. **Do things that energize you.** This is not as obvious as it sounds. It takes effort to recognize the activities that give you more energy both inside and outside of work. The real trick is consciously taking the time to do those things. Too many people fall into habits of convenience (such as, "Oh let's just watch another movie," instead of taking a walk through the woods). Track the things that fall into your leadership sweet spot. Track the things that energize you and the things that drain your energy. Doing this for a short time will provide insights that may surprise you.

2. **Manage the energy drains in your life.** Are there activities you do at work that seem exhausting? Are there people you sometimes interact with who just seem to drain your energy? Exceptional leaders are very aware of these and use various techniques to minimize the energy drains. Make a list of the drains and brainstorm ways you can counter their effects or reduce how frequently these occur. This may seem selfish but decreasing the energy drains and increasing your happiness and energy is a gift to everyone!

3. **Be prepared for energys dips.** The first two items are proactive actions you can take. Even with those actions clearly managed, there are times of the week, even during each day, when it feels that your energy has just fled. Be prepared. Carry your

favorite energy snacks. Hydrate. Take a brisk walk. Make some of your one-on-one meetings walking meetings. What are your best techniques?

4. **Give yourself the gift of empty spaces.** Some good managers are proud of being too busy to get enough sleep, to go for walks, or simply to pause and stare at a distant horizon. The exceptional leaders cherish these moments and work to create these spaces for themselves, often on a daily basis.

Some good managers believe it is a badge of honor to be tired and stressed, as it is an indicator of how hard they are working. Meanwhile, the exceptional leader is like organized lightning, with both a calming presence and an intensity that raises the whole energy of the situations they engage.

I know which leader I strive to be.

Which leader do the people around you think you are?

Take Control of Every Week

Hopefully, you see the wisdom of taking control of your leadership sweet spot and of supercharging your energy. To best be able to take control of those keys, you must take control of your time. The best way to do this is to have a regular planning process. I personally have a process for planning a very long period of time, such as a decade, one for planning my year, one for my month, and also one for planning my week.

If you can't control the time in your week, the rest won't matter. Your weekly personal planning process should focus on controlling (or at least greatly influencing) where the time in your week goes.

This example process has ten steps.

1. **Relax into the week.** Take time to consciously prepare your mindset for the week. It is useful for many people to have a key phrase or two to be a reminder of traits they are working on. For example, some leaders simply use this step to remind themselves how the week ahead is a choice of what things they choose to do and the attitude they bring to how they will do those things.

2. **Review and refresh upcoming family events.** Many leaders who have excelled at work find that they need to put family events first on their planning processes or they make costly mistakes in squeezing out some of the really important things in their lives. Look ahead at least two months and determine if there are any major things you want or need to do for the benefit of the family. Look at the upcoming week and think about family. Refresh in your mind upcoming events. Add any new events if needed. Note any actions taken at the end of your planning session.

3. **Look at your main upcoming work goals and events.** It is so easy to get pulled into the mundane of the day to day and lose track of where you really want to go. Look ahead. Think about your major goals. Think about major events. Note if there are any significant things you need to do this week.

4. **Review your calendar for the upcoming week.** Review the events already on your calendar. The upcoming week has almost certainly had more requests come in for your time via meetings or requests for you to do specific things. It may have grown over the weekend. Note which of the items are in your sweet spot and fit goals, which ones really don't, and which ones fall into a bit of a gray area. You don't need to decide yet!

5. **Consider your key stakeholders.** If you are a CEO or a project leader, you have key stakeholders who can help or hinder the initiatives you have in mind. Determine whether there is anyone you should contact this week to build momentum toward your goals.

6. **Take a moment to consider those you lead.** How is the group energy? Are there any spots that you are concerned about? Are there any people who could use some "trouble prevention" or "trouble correction" actions? Note that in all these steps you should be thinking about whether you can ask others to help you. Asking for help is one of the key steps for growing your leadership sweet spot.

7. **Consider the specific things you are working on.** Is progress on track? Is any extra effort needed in key spots? Should you be asking for help in any areas?

8. **List the most important positive impacts you will have this week.** Think about the positive impact you plan to make this week. Think about how to make that impact with the least amount of effort and time. Focus on value and return on investment of your time. Make the list realistic for the week based on the most important areas. It is great to add stretch goals. Even with those stretch goals, ensure that you are leaving open space on your calendar for those things that will come up.

9. **Make your list of "No, that will not happen" and either send or prepare to provide your polite words of "No thank you."** Again, this may sound selfish, but saying "no" to obligatory meetings or to less important meetings is not selfish. You are focused on energizing yourself and your organization. The exceptional leader accepts the reality that all of your "to do items" will not fit in a week. You also know that you can have a positive impact every day.

10. **Plan how to start the week with great momentum.** Start every week with a quick win that makes a positive impact. It helps others and gets the week started in the absolute right direction. It is more likely to happen when you plan for that to happen!

This list may seem like it will take more than one hour. Leaders who do this for the first time discover that it does take more time. The challenge is getting a system in place that helps keep the most important things in mind. Further, you may need to train others in your organization about how you have updated how you "own" your week.

After the start-up period, it takes less than an hour. The return on your energy is well worth that time!

Improve Your Ability to Improve

Two years ago I gave a speech to an audience of about 200. Afterwards, I had a nice line of people coming up to ask me some detailed questions. The last person asked me a question that made me laugh out loud after I understood it. She said: "How did you do that?" I thought she meant the stellar results I had helped an organization achieve, which was the focus of my talk. She explained more. She wanted to know "How did you give a speech where you were so comfortable, were interactive with the audience, answered questions the whole time, still hit all the important points, finished on time, and made me laugh?"

This made me laugh out loud for a couple of reasons. First, I am not sure that the guy who fell asleep in the third row, fourth from the left, about eight minutes in and didn't wake up until the final applause felt the same way! I also laughed because I still remembered my first public speech, which was a mess, both in content and in my sweaty panic.

The quick answer I gave was simply, "I decided to become excellent at giving talks. That is the best place to start." After I made that big decision, I started to work at it. I am now very comfortable at giving talks, and I do feel confident that they are usually good.

However, I am not done working on this skill. I will get better, and I have specific plans on what things I will do to accelerate that improvement.

The reason I am confident that I will get better is that the skill I have been really working to master is how to accelerate my ability to improve at anything!

Improving your skill at "how" to improve is the most powerful of all skills to master. Improving your ability to improve leads to making your leadership sweet spot bigger and more powerful. It leads to higher-level energizing partnerships. It leads to improvement in all areas.

The exceptional leader looks at all the problems and obstacles he faces. He thinks about what the common denominator is for all those problems. He looks in the mirror and smiles because he knows that common denominator is him.

The exceptional leader knows that he has the ability to improve.

And we can all improve in that skill. The following are the keys to taking ownership of accelerating your ability to improve.

▶ **Start with a clear intention and belief.** If you have something that you want to improve at, decide to get better. Believe that you are absolutely capable of getting better. Better yet, believe that because of your intention, you are already better just by being aware of the need, and having the desire. Write down your goals for getting better and why it is important to you.

▶ **Determine some indicators of success.** Your intention will be made much stronger by thinking about what it means to be better and asking yourself "How will I know that I am better?" When I decided to get better at giving public speeches I had a few simple ways to know if I had actually improved. For example, in the first speech I gave, I saw people quietly (and not so quietly) slipping out the back doors of the room. In more recent speeches, I have had people tell me that others had texted them to come see my talk, which was already in progress. It is important to have external indicators that you indeed are improving in the direction you desire.

▶ **Decide what things you will do differently.** And then, do those things differently. Doing the same thing the same way over and over again will get very similar results. So, when you decide to get better at something, think about what things you will actually change and what things you will try. You can do this immediately, even without a mentor or by reading a book. I am going to recommend those, but there is no good reason I can think of to wait unless you are parachuting or racing cars or the like!

▶ **Learn from success and from successful failures.** Celebrate both. Successful failures are failed attempts where you learned something. Note that also means you could have failed successes, in that you didn't learn why you were successful. So keep learning. Celebrate both! The better you get at celebrating failures the faster you will learn.

▶ **Watch others, both the good and the bad.** As soon as I decided to get great at giving speeches, it changed my speech-watching habits completely. I paid more attention to all the speeches I went to—the good and the bad. I made notes about each and why I thought they were good or bad. This gathering of experience helped me accelerate my progress immensely.

▶ **Find exceptional mentors.** Seek people who are better than you are and ask how they mastered that which you wish to master. If they seem to be a good fit, ask them for their help. How do you find a good mentor? Read books and write to the authors. Ask others who you see are good at what you want to improve at. Talk to them. Get their advice.

▶ **Create safe places to try new methods.** If you have no fear any place can be safe. However, I think it is still a good idea to have a testing ground. You can role-play with trusted peers. Or you can seek a community of people pursuing a similar quest to improve. For example, Toastmasters is a community where many find a safe place to improve at giving speeches. You can create your own safe place by accepting that you can make mistakes and it is okay.

▶ **Be willing to make public mistakes.** If you are trying new methods, it is very possible that the first couple of times might feel awkward and might even look awkward. You might feel less competent. You will make mistakes even when you are good, so really don't worry about it. If you can accept that public mistake-making, you will be much more likely to learn, celebrate, and accelerate your improvement.

▶ **Treasure empty spaces.** Truly great ideas for improvement come when you have successfully emptied your mind from worries and distractions and enabled your mind to be open to new ideas that are hidden within you. Use meditation, long walks in nature, watching bad movies, heavy exercise, listening to great music, or anything that helps you be receptive to new ideas.

▶ **Relax into the joy of learning.** I remember vividly the first day my daughter learned to walk when she was about eighteen months old. Within two hours she was running barefoot across stones yelling "ow, ow, ow" and laughing the whole time.

Learning new things and doing things new ways can be itself a great reward *or* it can be a stressful trudge. Choose the joy path! Truly relax into the joy of learning new ways.

Take Ownership of Your Leadership: The Secret of Managing Up

If you have mastered all the items in this chapter, you most likely have also discovered this final secret. We go to work because we choose to. We work in the organizations we work in because we accepted positions there. No one forced us to do the work that we do. The person you really work for is you.

I find that the people who have truly accepted this idea deal with the most common difficulties in simple, eloquent ways. The following example provides a template for how to transform troublesome stakeholders above and beside you into tremendous collaborators.

The Case of Too Many Bosses

When you have multiple stakeholders, it is rare for those stakeholders to agree on what your top priority is. Managers doing this poorly react to whoever is the loudest on that day. The other poor reaction is to simply work harder. These are reactions based on fear of repercussions from taking ownership of personal leadership power.

The proper action is to recognize that if there is no agreement on your priorities, then the only one who is going to set them is you. The fact is, you are already doing that, even if it is based on the process of "who is the loudest." If you take ownership of this reality you can set the priorities and then publish what the priorities for the organization are.

The next step is to provide a way for new priorities to be set. Work with the multiple stakeholders so that they know the challenges each of the other stakeholders face. Provide a process for them to come to consensus on how they can change the priorities of the organization you lead. The final key to this is that you are one of the stakeholders for your organization. Take ownership of your leadership power.

It is your choice to make.

REFLECTION POINTS

Owning your personal leadership power is the most powerful tool you will ever have in transforming the troublesome to the tremendous.

Do you own your power of leadership? Consider the following questions.

1. Track the things you do for a month. How much of the time do you feel like you are working from your leadership sweet spot where you get more energy out of the activity then you put into it?

2. Do the people you work around look at you as "often overwhelmed and stressed" or more like "organized lightning"?

3. Do you generally take control of where your time goes? Are others getting great impact and value from the time you are spending?

4. Have you consciously worked to improve in any key areas? Do you have a process for improvement that you are improving?

5. What steps are you taking to improve your ownership of your leadership?

14

Closing Notes on Transforming the Troublesome to the Tremendous

I f you have had enough years in your career, it is almost certain that you have at one point played the role of a maverick, cynic, slacker, or diva. Perhaps you have been part of firefighting projects or on projects that were consistently late, often with quality issues. Perhaps people who have worked for you thought you provided too little or sometimes too much guidance, bordering on micromanagement.

I know that at various points I have played those roles. Fortunately, whenever I have been in those roles in the early part of my career, I had excellent leaders who provided me the wisdom, guidance, and sometimes firm direction of how to work toward excellence. I thank those leaders.

It is important to remember that we have most likely been the difficult person before. It does not mean that we ignore the problematic behaviors when they occur. It is helpful to remember that the guidance we have been provided in the past is the guidance we must be able to mindfully provide to others.

This is important. As managers, as leaders, we must never waiver in our obligation to the mission we are engaged in and the group we are leading. Our obligation is to the group as a whole, which means sometimes we must provide tough guidance to those who are hindering the progress of the whole.

To me, we also have an obligation to each of the individuals, including those troublesome ones, to provide guidance that comes from compassion and a willingness to help. I once gave heartfelt advice to an employee. He had a choice to improve or move. He did not choose to improve. I accepted that honesty, and the integrity of our friendship lasted beyond the working relationship. He called me about fifteen years later and said "Okay, Alan, I am ready to work with you to improve on the suggestions you had for me. I get it now."

Every time that there is a troublesome person or situation, it is an opportunity to help someone grow—and perhaps even ourselves. It is an opportunity to transform the troublesome to the tremendous.

For further insights, informations and offers please visit http://leadtheunleadable.com

INDEX